If you only knew what a
wonderful gift God has for you,
and who Jesus is, you would
ask Him for Living Water,
and He would give it.

LIVING

WATER

THE GOSPEL OF JOHN
with notes

D1252902

Logos 21 is a modern yet accurate translation in everyday English. It is not a paraphrase, but closely resembles the everyday Greek (called *Koiné* or common) in which John wrote this Gospel. The name *Logos 21* is to suggest our desire to bring God's Word (Greek *Logos*) into the 21st century. For more information about *Logos 21* see page 72.

Living Water
The Gospel of John—Logos 21 Version

Scripture text is from the Logos 21 Version, copyright © 1996 by Arthur L. Farstad.

All material other than Scripture text
Copyright © 1996
Absolutely Free Incorporated

LW-L21-Pr12-US-12/00-Rev3

INTRODUCTORY NOTES

John: The Gospel of Belief

The Bible is the greatest work of literature, the most accurate record of ancient history, and the most profound book ever written. Great men and women of history have looked to the Scriptures for inspiration, guidance, and hope.

Napoleon wrote, "The Bible is no mere book, but a Living Creature, with a power that conquers all that opposes it."

George Washington said, "It is impossible to rightly govern the world without God and the Bible."

Abraham Lincoln believed that "the Bible is the best gift God has ever given to men. All the good from the Savior of the world is communicated to us through this book."

Of the 66 books of the Bible, this one, the Gospel of John, is the most loved. John 3:16 is regarded by many as the most important verse in the Bible: "For God so loved the world that He gave His only begotten Son, so that whoever believes in Him will not perish, but have eternal life."

This great book contains the most familiar, memorized, and quoted words of Scripture.

Why? Because this is the one book in God's Word written primarily to those who have not yet believed in Jesus Christ. While the rest of the Bible speaks mainly to those who know Christ, John has in mind those who do not know

Him. As an eyewitness to the events of Jesus' life, John selects the most convincing words and works of the One who claimed to be the Son of God and presents them to those who need eternal life:

"Jesus actually performed many other miraculous signs in the presence of His disciples, which are not written in this book. But these are written so that you may believe that Jesus is the Christ, the Son of God, and that by believing you may have life in His Name" (John 20:30-31).

John reveals that Jesus is the long-promised and long-awaited Christ, the Messiah of Israel, God's Son and Savior of the world. He is the Lamb of God who takes away the sin of the world. And He promises eternal life to everyone who believes this claim.

The emphasis throughout is on this free gift of eternal life offered to those who believe. Almost every chapter contains both an invitation to believe and a reason to believe in Jesus as the Christ, the Savior. In fact, the word *believe* occurs nearly 100 times to reinforce this main point.

So, for many believers in Jesus Christ, John's Gospel was their first exposure to the life-changing truths of God's Word. It was from these pages that God quenched their thirst for living water, the eternal life Christ offers to those who will receive it. No wonder Christians love this book so! It is God's inspired introduction to His Son. This is a book which leads to the faith in God's Son which brings eternal life.

Life's Most Important Question

What must I do to have eternal life? That's the most important question you will ever ask.

As you read through this Gospel you will find that eternal life comes not by doing, but by believing: …"Whoever believes in Me has eternal life" (John 6:47).

John will give you plenty of reasons to believe. You will read of seven miraculous signs, or miracles, which point to the fact that Jesus is the Son of God (chapters 1–12). Then, you will marvel at the compassion and wisdom of Jesus as He teaches His disciples on their last night together before His death (chapters 13–17). Finally, you will stand in wonder at the foot of the Cross, as Christ dies for the sins of the world, and then later rises from the dead, just as He had predicted (chapters 18–21; compare chapter 2, verse 19). And throughout, you will find men, women, boys, and girls just like you, everyday people with everyday problems, putting their faith in Jesus. They will conclude that Jesus is who He claimed to be, "the Savior of the world, the Christ!" (John 4:42).

Read the verses carefully and thoughtfully. We have provided a few helps to assist you as you read. Keep in mind that this book is *God's* answer to life's most important question, "How can I have eternal life?" Regardless of what some people may say, Jesus offers the free gift of eternal life to all who believe.

Our prayer is that your response will be to receive God's gift through faith, believing in God's Son. Faith, or belief, means *trust*. The moment you trust in Jesus as the One who is the Christ, the One who gives eternal life freely, eternal life is yours, just as He promised.

When you have answered life's most important question for yourself, you will want to turn to page 69 of this booklet for some further guidance concerning your belief in Christ and your new life in Him.

The notes to the verses marked * are on pages 73–75.

The Gospel According to St. John

IN the beginning was the Word,
and the Word was with God,
and the Word was God.

² He was in the beginning with God.
³ All things were made through Him,
and apart from Him
not one thing was made
that has been made.
⁴ In Him was Life
and the Life was the Light of men.
⁵ And the Light shines in the darkness,
yet the darkness did not grasp it.

⁶ A man appeared, sent from God,
whose name was John.
⁷ He came to give testimony,
to testify about the Light,
so that all might believe through him.
⁸ *He* was not the Light
but he came to testify about the Light.
⁹ That was the true Light
which gives light to everyone
who comes into the world.
¹⁰ He was in the world,
and the world was made through Him,
yet the world did not know Him.

¹¹ He came to His own,
 and His own people did not accept Him.
¹² But to as many as did accept Him,
 He gave the right to be God's children,
 to those who believed in His Name,
¹³ who were born,
 not of blood,
 nor of the will of the flesh,
 nor of the will of man,
 but of God.
¹⁴ And the Word became flesh
 and lived among us,
 and we saw His glory,
 glory as of the Father's Only-begotten,
 full of grace and truth.
¹⁵ John testified concerning Him and exclaimed,
 "This was the One of whom I said,
  'The One coming after me ranks ahead of me,
 because He was before me.'
¹⁶ And from His fullness we have all received,
 yes, grace upon grace.
¹⁷ For the law was given through Moses;
 grace and truth came through Jesus Christ.
¹⁸ No one has ever seen God.
 The only begotten Son,*
 who is nearest to the Father's heart—
 He has made Him known."

John 1:12-13. These verses are talking about those who responded to Jesus' call to believe in Him. (See John 2:11, 2:23, 3:36, 4:42, 4:53, 6:68-69, 10:42, 11:45, 12:42-43.)

Each and every person who received the Lord Jesus Christ by believing "in His Name" became a child of God. When they believed His claims about His Name, that He was the Christ, the Savior of man, they were receiving Him. The result of believing was that they were, at that moment, born of God. That is, they were given God's life (eternal life) and were born into His family.

And nothing has changed since John wrote these words. Anyone who will receive Jesus Christ by believing in His Name becomes a child of God.

JOHN THE BAPTIST'S TESTIMONY

[19] Now this is John's testimony when the Jews sent priests and Levites from Jerusalem to ask him,

"Who are *you*?"

[20] And he confessed, he did not deny, but confessed,

"*I* am not the Christ."

[21] "What then?" they asked him. "Are you Elijah?"

"I am not," he said.

"Are you *the Prophet*?"

"No," he answered.

[22] So they said to him,

"Who are you? —so that we can answer those who sent us. What do you have to say for yourself?"

[23] He said,

"I am *'the voice of one crying out:*

"Make a straight road in the desert for the Lord" '—just as the prophet Isaiah said."

[24] Now those who had been sent were from the Pharisees. [25] So they asked him,

"Why then do you baptize if you are not the Christ, or Elijah, or the Prophet?"

[26] John answered them,

"I baptize with water, but among you stands Someone you do not know. [27] *He* is the One coming after me, who ranks ahead of me, whose sandal strap I am not worthy to untie!"

[28] These things took place in Bethany, across the Jordan, where John was baptizing.

THE LAMB OF GOD

[29] The next day John saw Jesus coming toward him and said,

"Look! The Lamb of God, who takes away the sin of the world!

John 1:29. John the Baptist, a prophet from God, proclaims Jesus to be "the Lamb of God who takes away the sin of the world." This refers to Jesus' mission from God the Father. Jesus came to earth to die on the Cross for the sins of the entire world so that believers in Him could obtain eternal life.

By dying on the Cross Jesus did for us what we could not do for ourselves: He solved our sin problem.

³⁰ This is the One I told you about: 'After me comes a man who ranks ahead of me, because He was before me.' ³¹ Yet I did not know Him. However, the reason I came baptizing with water is that He might be made known to Israel."

³² And John testified,

"I observed the Spirit coming down like a dove out of Heaven. And He rested upon Him. ³³ Yet I did not know Him. However, He who sent me to baptize with water told me, 'The One on whom you see the Spirit coming down and resting—this is He who will baptize with the Holy Spirit.' ³⁴ So I have both seen and testified that this is the Son of God!"

³⁵ Again, the next day, John was standing with two of his disciples. ³⁶ And when he saw Jesus passing by, he said,

"Look! The Lamb of God!"

³⁷ So the two disciples heard him say this, and they followed Jesus.

³⁸ When Jesus turned and noticed them following Him He said,

"What are you looking for?"

And they said to Him,

"Rabbi" (which is translated Teacher), "Where are you staying?"

³⁹ "Come and see," He told them. They went and saw where He was staying, and they stayed with Him that day. It was about ten a.m.

⁴⁰ One of the two who heard John and followed Jesus was Andrew, Simon Peter's brother. ⁴¹ He first found his own brother, Simon, and told him,

"We have found the Messiah!" (which is translated Christ). ⁴² And he brought him to Jesus. When Jesus saw him, He said,

"*You* are Simon, son of Jonah.* *You* shall be called Cephas" (which is translated Peter).

PHILIP AND NATHANAEL

⁴³ The next day Jesus decided to leave for Galilee. So He found Philip and told him,

"Follow Me!"

⁴⁴ Now Philip was from Bethsaida, the hometown of Andrew and Peter. ⁴⁵ Philip found Nathanael and told him,

"We have found the One of whom Moses in the Law—and also the Prophets—wrote: Jesus the son of Joseph from Nazareth!"

[46] So Nathanael said to him,

"Can anything good come out of *Nazareth?*"

"Come and see!" Philip told him.

[47] Jesus saw Nathanael coming toward Him and said of him,

"This really is an Israelite in whom there is no deceit!"

[48] "How do you know me?" Nathanael asked Him.

In response, Jesus told him,

"Before Philip called you, when you were under the fig tree, I saw you."

[49] Nathanael answered Him,

"Rabbi, *You* are the Son of God! *You* are the King of Israel!"

[50] Replying, Jesus said to him,

"Because I told you I saw you under the fig tree, do you believe? You will see greater things than these!"

[51] And He said to him, "Amen, amen,* I tell you, in the future you will see Heaven opened and the angels of God ascending and descending upon the Son of Man!"

WATER INTO WINE

2 On the third day a wedding took place in Cana of Galilee. Now Jesus' mother was there. [2] Jesus and His disciples were also invited to the wedding. [3] So when the wine ran out, Jesus' mother told Him,

"They don't have any wine!"

[4] Jesus said to her, "Woman, how does that concern Me and you? My time has not yet come."

[5] "Do whatever He tells you," His mother told the servants.

[6] Now there were six stone water jars set there for Jewish purification. Each contained 20 or 30 gallons.

[7] "Fill up the jars with water," Jesus told them. So they filled them to the brim. [8] Then He said to them, "Now draw some out and take it to the master of ceremonies." So they took it.

[9] Now when the master of ceremonies had tasted the water (after it had become wine), and didn't know where it came from—though the servants who had drawn the water knew—he called the bridegroom [10] and told him,

"Everybody sets out the fine wine first, then, after people are intoxicated, the inferior, but you have kept the fine wine until now!"

¹¹ This first of His miraculous signs Jesus performed in Cana of Galilee, and thus displayed His glory. And His disciples believed in Him.

¹² After this He—with His mother, His brothers, and His disciples—went down to Capernaum, but they did not stay there many days.

CLEANING OUT THE TEMPLE COURTS

¹³ Now the Jewish Passover was near, so Jesus went up to Jerusalem. ¹⁴ And in the temple courts He found people selling oxen, sheep, and doves, and also the money changers sitting there. ¹⁵ So He made a whip out of cords and drove everyone out of the temple courts, with the sheep and the oxen. He also poured out the money changers' coins and tipped over the tables. ¹⁶ Then, to those who were selling doves, He said,

"Get these things out of here! Stop turning my Father's house into a marketplace!"

¹⁷ And His disciples remembered that it is written:

"Zeal for Your house will consume Me!"

¹⁸ So in reply the Jews said to Him,

"What miraculous sign do You show us, since You do these things?"

¹⁹ Jesus answered them,

"Destroy this sanctuary and I will raise it up in three days!"

²⁰ Therefore the Jews said,

"This sanctuary took 46 years to build, and will *You* raise it up in three days?"

²¹ But *He* was talking about the sanctuary of His body. ²² So when He was raised from the dead His disciples remembered that He had said this. And they believed the Scripture and the statement that Jesus had made.

²³ Now while He was in Jerusalem at the Passover festival, many believed in His Name when they observed the miraculous signs He was performing. ²⁴ Jesus, however, would not trust

Himself to them, since He knew all men [25] and didn't need anyone to testify about a man; for He Himself knew what was in a man.

JESUS AND NICODEMUS

3 But there was a man from the Pharisees named Nicodemus, a ruler of the Jews. [2] This man came to Him at night and said to Him,

"Rabbi, we know that You have come as a teacher from God, because no one can perform these miraculous signs You do unless God is with him."

[3] Replying, Jesus said to him,

"Amen, amen,* I tell you, unless one is born again, he cannot see the kingdom of God."

[4] Nicodemus asked Him,

"How can anyone be born when he is old? He can't enter his mother's womb a second time and be born, can he?"

[5] Jesus answered,

"Amen, amen, I tell you, unless one is born of water and the Spirit, he cannot enter the kingdom of God. [6] That which is born of the flesh is flesh, and that which is born of the Spirit is spirit. [7] Don't be amazed that I told you, 'You all must be born again.' [8] The wind blows where it will, and you hear its sound, but you don't know where it is coming from and where it is going. So it is with everyone who is born of the Spirit."

[9] In response Nicodemus said to Him,

"How can these things be?"

[10] Jesus answered him,

"Are *you* a teacher of Israel and don't know these things? [11] Amen, amen, I tell you, We speak what We know and We testify to what We have seen, but you all reject Our testimony. [12] If I have told you earthly things and you don't believe, how will you believe if I tell you heavenly things? [13] Now no one has ascended into Heaven except the One who descended from Heaven—the Son of Man, who is in Heaven.* [14] And just as Moses lifted up the serpent in the desert, likewise the Son of Man must be lifted up, [15] so that whoever believes in Him will not perish, but have eternal life.

¹⁶ "For God so loved the world that He gave His only begotten Son, so that whoever believes in Him should not perish, but have eternal life. ¹⁷ For God did not send His Son into the world to judge the world, but that the world might be saved through Him. ¹⁸ Whoever believes in Him is not judged, but whoever does not believe is already judged, because he has not believed in the Name of the only begotten Son of God.

¹⁹ "And this is the judgment, that the Light has come into the world, and people loved darkness rather than the Light, because their deeds were evil. ²⁰ In fact, everyone who does wicked things hates the Light and doesn't come to the Light, so that his deeds may not be exposed. ²¹ But he who does the truth comes to the Light, so it may be clear that his deeds have been accomplished in God."

JESUS AND JOHN THE BAPTIST

²² After these things Jesus and His disciples went to the Judean countryside, where He spent time with them and baptized. ²³ Now John also was baptizing in Ainon, near Salem, because there was plenty of water there. And people were coming and being baptized, ²⁴ since John had not yet been thrown into prison.

²⁵ Then a dispute arose between John's disciples and a Judean about purification. ²⁶ So they came to John and told him:

"Rabbi, the One who was with you across the Jordan, of whom you testified, here He is baptizing, and everyone is flocking to Him!"

²⁷ John answered,

"A person can receive nothing unless it is given to him from Heaven. ²⁸ You yourselves can testify that I said, '*I am not the Christ, but I have been sent ahead of Him.*' ²⁹ He who has the bride is the bridegroom. But the bridegroom's friend, who stands

---

John 3:16. This is probably the most quoted verse in the Bible. The reason for its popularity is clear. It gives God's way of salvation in a nutshell. God loved us so much He sent His Son to die on the Cross for our sins. As a result, when we believe in His Son, we will never perish in hell but will possess eternal life forever.

by and listens to him, has great joy at the bridegroom's voice. So this joy of mine is complete.

[30] "He must increase, but I must decrease. [31] The One who comes from above is above all. The one who is from the earth is earthly and talks in an earthly way. The One who comes from Heaven is above all. [32] And He testifies to what He has seen and heard, yet no one accepts His testimony. [33] Anyone who has accepted His testimony has certified that God is true. [34] For He whom God sent speaks God's words, since God gives the Spirit without measure.

[35] "The Father loves the Son and has given everything into His hands. [36] Whoever believes in the Son has eternal life; but whoever disbelieves the Son will not see life, but God's wrath remains upon him."

JESUS AND THE SAMARITAN WOMAN

4 So when the Lord knew that the Pharisees had heard that He was making and baptizing more disciples than John ([2] though in fact, Jesus Himself was not baptizing, but His disciples) [3] He left Judea and went away to Galilee.

[4] Now He had to pass through Samaria, [5] and He came to a town of Samaria called Sychar. It was near the plot of land which Jacob had given to his son Joseph, [6] and Jacob's Well was there. Therefore, Jesus, being worn out from the journey, sat by the well, just as He was. It was about six p.m.

[7] A woman of Samaria came out to draw water.

"Give Me a drink," Jesus told her. ([8] For His disciples had gone into town to buy food.)

[9] So the Samaritan woman said to Him, "How is it that You, a Jew, ask a drink from *me*, a Samaritan woman?" (For Jews do not associate with Samaritans.)

[10] Jesus answered her,

"If you knew the gift of God, and who it is that is saying to you, 'Give Me a drink,' you would have asked Him, and He would have given you living water!"

[11] "Sir," the woman said to Him, "You don't even have a bucket and the well is deep. So where do you get this 'living water'? [12] You aren't greater than our ancestor Jacob, are you? He gave us

the well and drank from it himself, as did his sons and his cattle."

¹³ In response Jesus told her,

"Everyone who drinks from this water will be thirsty again. ¹⁴ But whoever drinks from the water that I will give him will never thirst again—forever! On the contrary, the water that I will give him will become within him a spring of water gushing up to eternal life."

¹⁵ "Sir," the woman said to Him, "give me this water so that I won't get thirsty or come here to draw."

¹⁶ "Go call your husband," Jesus told her, "and come back here."

¹⁷ "I don't have a husband," the woman replied.

"You have rightly said, 'I don't have a *husband*,'" Jesus told her. ¹⁸ "Actually, you've had five husbands, and the one you have now is not *your* husband. You've spoken the truth there!"

¹⁹ "Sir," the woman told Him, "I see that You are a prophet. ²⁰ Our ancestors worshiped on this mountain, yet you Jews say the place where a person ought to worship is in Jerusalem."

²¹ "Woman," Jesus told her, "believe Me, a time is coming when you will not worship the Father either on this mountain or in Jerusalem. ²² You Samaritans worship what you do not know. *We* worship what we do know, because salvation is from the Jews. ²³ But a time is coming, and is now here, when the true worshipers will worship the Father in spirit and truth. Yes, the Father is looking for such people to worship Him. ²⁴ God is Spirit, and those who worship Him must worship in spirit and truth."

²⁵ The woman said to Him,

"I know that Messiah is coming" (who is called Christ). "Whenever *He* comes, He will explain everything to us."

²⁶ "I am He," Jesus told her, "the very One who is speaking to you."

John 4:14. The *water of life* is the wonderful truth that Jesus is the Christ who gives salvation to every believer (see verses 25,26,42). This truth produces in the believer a "spring" from which flows eternal life. Since that life lasts forever, no one who takes this living water will ever get thirsty, that is, need eternal life again.

One drink of the living water Jesus offers quenches a person's thirst for everlasting life. God's gift of eternal life is permanent and cannot be lost.

THE RIPENED HARVEST

²⁷ Just then His disciples came, and they were amazed that He was talking with a woman. Yet no one said, "What do You want?" or, "Why are You talking with her?"

²⁸ Then the woman left her water jar, went into town, and told the men,

²⁹ "Come, see a man who told me everything I ever did! Could this be the Christ?"

³⁰ They left the town and made their way toward Him.

³¹ Now in the meantime the disciples were urging Him,

"Rabbi, eat something."

³² But He said to them,

"I have food to eat that you don't know about."

³³ So the disciples said to one another,

"Could someone have brought Him something to eat?"

³⁴ "My food," Jesus told them, "is to do the will of Him who sent Me and to finish His work. ³⁵ Don't you say, 'There are still four more months, then comes harvest'? Look, I tell you, raise your eyes and observe the fields: they are white for harvest already! ³⁶ And the reaper receives pay and gathers fruit for eternal life, so that both the sower and the reaper can be glad together. ³⁷ For there is a true saying about this: 'One sows and another reaps.' ³⁸ I sent you to reap what you didn't labor for. Others have labored and you have entered into their labor."

THE SAVIOR OF THE WORLD

³⁹ Now many Samaritans from that town believed in Him because of what the woman reported when she testified, "He told me everything I ever did!" ⁴⁰ Therefore, when the Samaritans came to Him, they asked Him to stay with them. So He stayed there two days. ⁴¹ Then many more believed because of what He said. ⁴² So they told the woman,

"We no longer believe because of what *you* said, since we've heard Him ourselves and know that this really is the Savior of the world, the Christ!"

A GALILEAN WELCOME

⁴³ But after those two days He left there and went to Galilee. ⁴⁴ For Jesus Himself had testified that a prophet has no honor in his own country. ⁴⁵ Therefore, when they entered Galilee, the Galileans welcomed Him because they had seen everything which He did in Jerusalem during the festival. For they too had gone to the festival.

HEALING AN OFFICIAL'S SON

⁴⁶ So Jesus went again to Cana of Galilee, where He had turned the water into wine. Now there was a certain royal official whose son was ill at Capernaum. ⁴⁷ When this man heard that Jesus had come out of Judea into Galilee, he went to Him and implored Him to come down and heal his son, since he was about to die.

⁴⁸ So Jesus told him,

"Unless you people see miraculous signs and wonders, you will *not* believe."

⁴⁹ "Sir," the official said to him, "come down before my boy dies!"

⁵⁰ "Go," Jesus told him, "your son has recovered." So the man believed the statement Jesus made to him and started on his journey. ⁵¹ And while he was still going down, his servants met him and announced,

"Your boy has recovered!"

⁵² So he asked them at what time he got better. They told him,

"Yesterday at seven o'clock the fever left him."

⁵³ Then the father realized that this was the very time at which Jesus had told him, "Your son has recovered." And he himself believed, and so did his whole household.

⁵⁴ Now this was a second miraculous sign Jesus performed after He came from Judea to Galilee.

THE POOL OF BETHESDA

5 After these things there was a Jewish festival, and Jesus went up to Jerusalem. ² Now by the Sheep Gate in Jerusalem there is a pool, called Bethesda* in Hebrew, which has five colonnades. ³ Around these lay a great number of invalids—blind people, lame

people, people with shriveled limbs—waiting for the moving of the water, [4] because an angel would go down into the pool from time to time and stir up the water. Then the first one who went in after the water was stirred up recovered from whatever ailment he had.*

[5] Now there was a certain man there who had been an invalid for 38 years. [6] When Jesus saw him lying there and knew that he had already been there a long time, He said to him,

"Do you want to get well?"

[7] "Sir," the man answered Him, "I have no man to put me into the pool when the water is stirred up, but while I'm coming, someone else goes down before me."

[8] "Get up," Jesus told him, "pick up your bedroll and walk!" [9] Immediately the man got well and picked up his bedroll and started to walk. [10] Now that day was the Sabbath. So the Jews said to the man who had been healed,

"It's the Sabbath! You're not permitted to pick up your bedroll."

[11] He answered them,

"The man who made me well—He told me, 'Pick up your bedroll and walk.'"

[12] So they asked him,

"Who is the man who told you, 'Pick up your bedroll and walk?'" [13] But the man who was cured did not know who it was, for Jesus had slipped away, since there was a crowd in that place.

[14] After these things Jesus found him in the temple courts and said to him,

"See, you are well. Don't sin any more, so that something worse doesn't happen to you." [15] The man went away and reported to the Jews that it was Jesus who had made him well.

HONOR THE FATHER AND THE SON

[16] Therefore the Jews began persecuting Jesus and trying to kill Him, because He was doing these things on the Sabbath.

[17] But Jesus answered them,

"My Father has been working until now, and I have been working." [18] So for this reason the Jews were trying all the harder to kill

Him, because not only was He breaking the Sabbath, but He was even calling God His own Father, making Himself equal with God.

[19] In reply, therefore, Jesus said to them,

"Amen, amen,* I tell you, the Son is not able to do anything by Himself, but only what He sees the Father doing. For whatever *He* does, these things the Son also does in the same way. [20] For the Father loves the Son and shows Him everything which He is doing, and He will show Him *greater deeds* than these, so that you will be amazed. [21] For just as the Father raises the dead and gives them life, so also the Son gives life to whom He wishes. [22] The Father, in fact, does not judge anyone, but He has given all judgment to the Son, [23] so that all people will honor the Son just as they honor the Father. Whoever does not honor the Son does not honor the Father who sent Him.

LIFE AND JUDGMENT

[24] "Amen, amen, I tell you, whoever hears My word and believes the One who sent Me has eternal life, and will not come into judgment, but has passed from death to life.

[25] "Amen, amen, I tell you, a time is coming, and is now here, when the dead will hear the voice of the Son of God, and those who hear will live. [26] For just as the Father has life in Himself, so He has granted the Son also to have life in Himself. [27] He has granted Him the added authority to pass judgment, because He is the Son of Man. [28] Don't be amazed at this, because a time is coming in which all who are in the graves will hear His voice [29] and will come out: those who have done good things, to the resurrection of life; but those who have done wicked things, to the resurrection of judgment.

[30] "I can do nothing by Myself. Just as I hear, I judge, and My judgment is just, because I do not seek My own will, but the will of the Father who sent Me.

John 5:24. "Amen, amen" is Jesus' way of saying to His hearers, "You can be sure of this!" (See note to 1:51, page 73.) Jesus promises eternal life and escape from judgment to all who will trust in God's word about Him. And what has God said? Verses 20 and 21 make it clear. God the Father sent Jesus the Son to give eternal life to all who believe.

FOUR WITNESSES TO JESUS

[31] "If I were to testify about Myself, My testimony would not be valid. [32] There is Another who testifies about Me, and I know that the testimony which He gives concerning Me is valid. [33] You have sent to John, and he has testified to the truth. [34] But I do not receive testimony from man. However, I say these things so that you may be saved. [35] That man was a burning and shining lamp, and for a time you were willing to be glad in his light.

[36] "But I have a greater testimony than John's, because the works which the Father gave Me to accomplish—these very works that I am doing—testify about Me, that the Father has sent Me.

[37] "Also, the Father who sent Me has Himself testified about Me. You have not heard His voice at any time, nor have you seen His form. [38] Also you do not have His word abiding in you, because you do not believe the One whom He sent. [39] You pore over the Scriptures because in them you think you have eternal life, and yet it is they which testify about Me. [40] But you aren't willing to come to Me to have life. [41] I do not accept praise from men. [42] But I know you, that you do not have the love of God in you. [43] I have come in My Father's Name, yet you don't accept Me. If someone else comes in his own name, you will accept *him*. [44] How can *you* believe, since you accept praise from one another and don't seek the praise which comes from the only God?

[45] "Do not think that *I* will accuse you to the Father. There is one who does accuse you—Moses, on whom you have set your hope! [46] For if you believed Moses, you would believe Me, because it was about Me that he wrote. [47] But if you don't believe *his writings*, how will you believe *My words?*"

FEEDING OF THE FIVE THOUSAND

6 After these things Jesus crossed the Sea of Galilee (Tiberias). [2] And a huge crowd was following Him because they saw His miraculous signs that He performed on the sick. [3] And Jesus went up on a mountain and sat down there with His disciples.

[4] Now the Passover, a Jewish festival, was near. [5] Therefore, when Jesus looked up and saw a huge crowd coming toward Him, He said to Philip,

"Where shall we buy bread so that these people may eat?"
⁶ Now He said this to test him, for He Himself knew what He was about to do.

⁷ Philip answered Him,

"Two hundred denarii worth of bread wouldn't be enough for them, so each one of them could have a little."

⁸ One of His disciples, Andrew, Peter's brother, said to Him,

⁹ "There's a little boy here who has five barley loaves and two little fish—but what are they for so many?"

¹⁰ Nevertheless Jesus said,

"Have the men sit down." Now there was plenty of grass in the place. So the men sat down, about five thousand in number.
¹¹ Then Jesus took the loaves, and after giving thanks He distributed them to the disciples, and the disciples distributed them to those who were seated. So too with the fish, as much as they wanted.

¹² Now when they were full, He told His disciples,

"Collect the leftovers so that nothing is wasted." ¹³ Therefore they collected them and filled twelve baskets with fragments of the five barley loaves that were left over by those who had eaten.

¹⁴ Therefore, when the men saw the miraculous sign that Jesus had performed, they said,

"This man really is the Prophet who was to come into the world!"

WALKING ON WATER

¹⁵ Therefore, when Jesus knew that they were about to come and take Him by force to make Him king, He went away to the mountain by Himself.

¹⁶ Now when evening came His disciples went down to the sea, ¹⁷ and when they got into the boat they started to cross the sea to Capernaum. Darkness had already set in, yet Jesus had not come to them. ¹⁸ Then a high wind arose, and the sea began to churn. ¹⁹ So when they had rowed about three or four miles, they saw Jesus walking on the sea and coming near the boat. And they were afraid.

²⁰ But He said to them,

"It is I, don't be afraid!" [21] Then they were willing to take Him on board—and at once the boat was at the shore where they were heading.

THE BREAD OF LIFE

[22] The next day, the crowd which had stayed on the other side of the sea saw that there was no other boat there except the one in which His disciples had embarked. Also they saw that Jesus had not boarded the boat with His disciples, but His disciples had gone off alone. [23] However, other boats from Tiberias did come near the place where they ate the bread after the Lord had given thanks. [24] And when the crowd saw that neither Jesus nor His disciples were there, they also got into the boats and went to Capernaum, looking for Jesus. [25] And when they found Him on the other side of the sea, they said to Him,

"Rabbi, when did You get here?"

[26] Jesus answered them,

"Amen, amen,* I tell you, you're looking for Me, not because you saw the miraculous signs, but because you ate the bread and were satisfied. [27] Do not work for the food that perishes, but for the food that endures to eternal life, which the Son of Man will give you, because God the Father has set His seal of approval on Him."

[28] So they said to Him,

"What shall we do so that we may perform the works of God?"

[29] In reply Jesus told them,

"This is the work of God, that you believe in the One whom He has sent."

[30] So they said to Him,

"Then what miraculous sign are You going to do so we may see and believe You? What are You going to perform? [31] Our forefathers ate the manna in the desert, just as it is written:

'He gave them bread from Heaven to eat.'"

[32] So Jesus said to them,

"Amen, amen, I tell you, it was not Moses who gave you the bread from Heaven; but it is My Father who gives you the *true* bread from Heaven. [33] For the Bread of God is the One who came down from Heaven and gives life to the world."

[34] Then they said to Him,

"Sir, give us this bread always!"

[35] "I am the Bread of Life," Jesus told them. "Whoever comes to Me will never be hungry and whoever believes in Me will never, ever be thirsty. [36] But, as I told you, you've seen Me and yet don't believe. [37] All that the Father gives Me will come to Me, and the one who comes to Me I will never cast out. [38] For I have come down from Heaven, not to do *My* will, but the will of the One who sent Me. [39] Now this is the will of the Father who sent Me, that I shall lose none of all that He has given Me, but shall raise him up on the last day. [40] And this is the will of Him who sent Me, that everyone who sees the Son and believes in Him shall have eternal life, and I will raise him up on the last day."

A NEGATIVE REACTION

[41] Then the Jews started grumbling about Him, because He said, "I am the Bread that came down from Heaven." [42] And they were saying,

"Isn't this Jesus the son of Joseph, whose father and mother we know? So how can this man say, "I have come down *from Heaven*?"

[43] Therefore Jesus answered them,

"Stop grumbling among yourselves. [44] No one can come to Me unless the Father who sent Me draws him, and I will raise him up on the last day. [45] It is written in the Prophets: *'And they will all be taught by God.'* Therefore everyone who listens to the Father, and learns, comes to Me. [46] Not that anyone has seen the Father except the One who is from God—He has seen the Father.

[47] "Amen, amen, I tell you, whoever believes in Me* has eternal life. [48] I am the Bread of Life. [49] Your forefathers ate the manna in the desert, and they died. [50] This is the Bread that came down from Heaven so that one may eat of it and not die. [51] I am the

---

John 6:47. This is one of the clearest and simplest expressions of the Gospel, the Good News about Jesus Christ, in all of Scripture. Faith in Jesus brings eternal life to the believer. Notice that nothing is added to simple faith. There is no mention of baptism, surrender, church membership, or good works. If we *believe in Jesus*, we *have* eternal life.

living Bread which came down from Heaven. If anyone eats of this Bread he will live forever. And the Bread which I will give is My flesh, which I will give for the life of the world."

⁵² Then the Jews disputed among themselves, saying,

"How can this man give us His flesh to eat?"

⁵³ So Jesus told them,

"Amen, amen,* I tell you, if you do not eat the flesh of the Son of Man and drink His blood, you do not have life in yourselves. ⁵⁴ Whoever eats My flesh and drinks My blood has eternal life, and I will raise him up on the last day, ⁵⁵ because My flesh is true food, and My blood is true drink. ⁵⁶ Whoever eats My flesh and drinks My blood dwells in Me, and I in him. ⁵⁷ Just as the living Father sent Me, I also live because of the Father; and whoever eats of Me, he too will live because of Me. ⁵⁸ This is the Bread which came down from Heaven—not like the manna your forefathers ate; and they are dead. Whoever eats this Bread will live forever."

⁵⁹ He said these things while teaching in a synagogue in Capernaum.

DISCIPLES DESERTING

⁶⁰ Therefore, when many of His disciples heard this, they said,

"This teaching is hard! Who can listen to it?"

⁶¹ But Jesus, knowing in Himself that His disciples were grumbling about this, said to them:

"Does this offend you? ⁶² What then if you saw the Son of Man ascending to where He was before? ⁶³ The Spirit is the One who gives life. The flesh is of no profit at all. The words that I speak to you are spirit and are life. ⁶⁴ But there are some among you who don't believe." (For Jesus knew from the start who they were that didn't believe, and who it was that would betray Him.)

⁶⁵ So He said,

"This is why I told you that no one can come to Me unless it is granted to him by My Father."

⁶⁶ From that time many of His disciples turned back and no longer walked with Him. ⁶⁷ Therefore Jesus said to the Twelve,

"You don't want to go away too, do you?"

⁶⁸ Then Simon Peter said to Him,

"Lord, to whom shall we go? You have the words of eternal life. ⁶⁹ And we have come to believe and know that You are the Christ, the Son of the Living God!"

⁷⁰ Jesus answered them,

"Didn't *I* choose *you*, the Twelve? Yet one of you is a devil!" ⁷¹ He was referring to Judas Iscariot, the son of Simon, for he was going to betray Him, although he was one of the Twelve.

JESUS' BROTHERS DISBELIEVE

7 After these things Jesus moved about in Galilee, since He didn't want to travel in Judea because the Judeans were trying to kill Him. ² Now the Jewish festival of Tabernacles was near. ³ So His brothers said to Him,

"Leave here and go up to Judea so Your disciples can see the works which You are doing, ⁴ because no one does something in secret while he is actually seeking public notice. If You do these things, show Yourself to the world." ⁵ (For not even His brothers believed in Him.)

⁶ So Jesus told them,

"My time hasn't arrived yet, but *your* time is always at hand. ⁷ The world can't hate you, but it does hate Me because I testify about it—that its deeds are evil. ⁸ Go up to this festival yourselves. I'm not going up to this festival yet,* because My time has not yet fully come." ⁹ After He had said these things He stayed in Galilee.

JESUS TEACHES AT THE FESTIVAL OF TABERNACLES

¹⁰ Now when His brothers had gone up, then He too went up to the festival, not publicly, but as it were in secret.

¹¹ Therefore the Judeans were looking for Him at the festival and saying,

"Where is He?" ¹² And there was a lot of murmuring about Him among the crowds. Some were saying, "He's a good man." Others were saying, "No, on the contrary, He's deceiving the crowd." ¹³ Still, nobody was talking publicly about Him because they feared the Judeans.

¹⁴ Now when the festival was already half over, Jesus went up

into the temple courts and began to teach. [15] And the Judeans were astonished, saying,

"How does He know the Scriptures, since He hasn't been trained?"

[16] So in reply to them Jesus said,

"My teaching isn't Mine, but His who sent Me. [17] If anyone wants to do His will, he will know about the teaching, whether it is from God or if I am speaking on My own authority. [18] The person who speaks on his own authority is seeking his own glory. But He who is seeking the glory of the One who sent Him, He is true, and there is no no unrighteousness in Him. [19] Didn't Moses give you the law? And yet not one of you keeps the law! Why are you trying to kill Me?"

[20] The crowd replied,

"You've got a demon! Who's trying to kill You?"

[21] In response Jesus told them,

"I did one work, and you are all astonished. [22] This is why Moses has given you circumcision (not that it comes from Moses but from the patriarchs), and you circumcise a man on the Sabbath. [23] If a man receives circumcision on the Sabbath so that the Law of Moses won't be broken, are you angry at Me because I made an entire man healthy on the Sabbath? [24] Stop judging by outward appearance, but judge with right judgment."

COULD THIS BE THE CHRIST?

[25] So some of the Jerusalemites were saying:

"Isn't this the man they're trying to kill? [26] Yet look! He's speaking publicly and they're saying nothing to Him. It couldn't be true, could it, that the authorities know that He actually is the Christ? [27] But we know where this man is from. Yet whenever the Christ comes, nobody knows where He is from."

[28] Then, as He was teaching in the temple courts, Jesus cried out and said,

"Yes, you know Me, and you know where I am from. Yet I have not come on My own authority, but the One who sent Me, whom you do not know, is true. [29] I know Him because I am from Him, and He sent Me."

³⁰ Then they were trying to seize Him. Yet no one laid a hand on Him because His time had not yet come. ³¹ Many from the crowd, however, believed in Him and said,

"When the Christ comes He won't perform more miraculous signs than those which this man has done, will He?"

³² The Pharisees heard the crowd muttering these things about Him, so the Pharisees and the chief priests sent temple police to arrest Him.

³³ Therefore Jesus said:

"For a short time, I am still with you. Then I am going to the One who sent Me. ³⁴ You will look for Me and you will not find Me; and where *I* am *you* cannot come."

³⁵ So the Judeans said to one another,

"Where does He intend to go that *we* won't find Him? He doesn't intend to go to the Dispersion among the Greeks, and teach the Greeks, does He? ³⁶ What is this remark He made: 'You will look for Me and you will not find Me; and where *I* am *you* cannot come'?"

Jesus Promises the Holy Spirit

³⁷ Now on the last and most important day of the festival, Jesus stood up and cried out saying,

³⁸ "If anyone is thirsty, let him come to Me and drink. He who believes in Me, as the Scripture has said, from deep within him will flow streams of living water." ³⁹ (Now He said this about the Spirit, whom those who believed in Him were going to receive, for the Holy Spirit had not yet been given because Jesus had not yet been glorified.)

The People Divided over Jesus

⁴⁰ So when many from the crowd heard this statement they said,

"This really is the Prophet!"

⁴¹ Others said,

"This is the Christ."

Others said,

"Surely the Christ doesn't come from *Galilee*, does He? ⁴² Doesn't the Scripture say that the Christ comes from David's line and from the town of Bethlehem, where David lived?" [43] So there was division among the crowd because of Him. [44] Now some of them wanted to seize Him, but no one laid hands on Him.

THE LEADERS REJECT JESUS' CLAIM

[45] Then the temple police came to the chief priests and Pharisees, who said to them,

"Why haven't you brought Him?"

[46] The police answered,

"No man ever spoke like this man!"

[47] Then the Pharisees answered them,

"You aren't fooled too, are you? [48] None of the rulers have believed in Him, have they? Or any of the Pharisees? [49] But this mob that doesn't know the law is accursed!" [50] Nicodemus, the one who came to Him at night, who was one of them, said to them,

[51] "Our law doesn't judge a man before it hears from him and knows what he's doing, does it?"

[52] Replying, they said to him,

"You aren't from Galilee too, are you? Search and see: no prophet has ever arisen from Galilee."

[53] So each one went to his house.

8 And Jesus went to the Mount of Olives.

AN ADULTERESS FORGIVEN

[2] But at the break of dawn Jesus went to the temple courts again, and all the people were coming to Him. And He sat down and began to teach them.

[3] Then the scribes and the Pharisees brought to Him a woman caught in adultery. They made her stand in the center [4] and said to Him,

"Teacher, we found this woman in the very act of adultery. [5] Now in our law Moses commanded us to stone such women. So what do *You* say about her?"

[6] They said this to test Him, so that they might have an accusation against Him.

But Jesus stooped down and started to write on the ground with His finger. ⁷ So when they persisted in asking Him, He looked up and said to them,

"Let him who is without sin among you be the first to throw a stone at her!" ⁸ Then He stooped down again and wrote on the ground. ⁹ But when they heard this they went out one by one, starting with the older men down to the very last.

Only Jesus was left, with the woman in the center. ¹⁰ So when Jesus had straightened up, He saw her and said,

"Woman, where are your accusers? Has no one condemned you?"

¹¹ "No one, Lord," she said.

"Neither do I condemn you," Jesus told her. "Go, and don't sin any more."*

¹² So Jesus spoke to them again, saying,

"I am the Light of the world. Whoever follows Me will *not* walk in darkness, but will have the light of life."

JESUS' SELF-WITNESS

¹³ Then the Pharisees said to Him,

"*You* are testifying about Yourself. Your testimony is not valid."

¹⁴ In reply Jesus told them:

"Even if I testify about Myself, my testimony is valid, because I know where I came from and where I am going. But *you* don't know where I come from and where I am going. ¹⁵ *You* are judging by human standards. I am not judging anyone. ¹⁶ And even if I do judge, My judgment is valid, because I am not alone, but I and the Father who sent Me are together. ¹⁷ Even in *your* law it is written that the witness of two men is valid. ¹⁸ I am the One who testifies concerning Myself, and the *Father* who sent Me testifies concerning Me."

¹⁹ Then they said to Him,

"Where is Your Father?"

"You know neither Me nor My Father," Jesus replied. "If you knew Me, you would also know My Father." ²⁰ Jesus spoke these words in the treasury, while teaching in the temple courts. Yet no one seized Him, because His time had not yet come.

JESUS PREDICTS HIS DEPARTURE

[21] Then Jesus said to them again,

"I am going away, and you will look for Me, but you will die in your sin. Where I am going *you* cannot come."

[22] So the Jews said again,

"He isn't going to kill Himself, is He, since He says, 'Where I am going *you* cannot come'?"

[23] "*You* are from below," He told them. "*I* am from above. *You* are of this world, *I* am not of this world. [24] Therefore I told you that you would die in your sins. For if you do not believe that I am He, you will die in your sins."

[25] So they said to Him,

"Who are You?"

"Precisely what I've been telling you from the very beginning," Jesus told them. [26] "I have many things to say about you and to judge, but the One who sent Me is true, and what I have heard from Him—these things I tell the world."

[27] They didn't know that He was speaking to them about the Father. [28] So Jesus said to them,

"When you lift up the Son of Man, then you will know that I am He, and by Myself I do nothing. But just as My Father taught Me, these things I speak. [29] And the One who sent Me is with Me. The Father has not left Me alone, because I always do the things that please Him."

THE TRUTH WILL MAKE YOU FREE

[30] As He was saying these things many believed in Him. [31] So Jesus said to those Jews who had believed Him,

"If you abide in My word, you really are My disciples. [32] And you will know the truth, and the truth will set you free."

[33] "We are descendants of Abraham," they answered Him, "and we have *never* been enslaved to anyone. How can You say, 'You will be set free'?"

[34] Jesus answered them,

"Amen, amen,* I tell you, whoever commits sin is a slave of sin. [35] A slave does not remain in the household forever, but a son does remain forever. [36] Therefore if the Son sets you free, you really will be free. ³⁷ I know that you are descendants of Abraham, but you are trying to kill Me because My word finds no place in you. ³⁸ I speak what I have seen in the presence of My Father, and you in turn do what you have seen in company with your father."

³⁹ In reply they said to Him,

"Our father is Abraham!"

"If you were Abraham's children," Jesus told them, "you would do Abraham's deeds. ⁴⁰ But now you are trying to kill Me, a man who has told you the truth which I heard from God. Abraham didn't do this! ⁴¹ *You* are doing the deeds of your father."

Then they said to Him,

"*We* were not born of fornication; we have one Father—God."

⁴² So Jesus said to them,

"If God were your Father, you would love Me, because I came forth from God and I am here. For I have not come by My own authority, but He sent Me. ⁴³ Why don't you understand what I say? Because you are not able to listen to My word. ⁴⁴ *You* are of your father the devil, and you want to do your father's desires. *He* was a murderer from the beginning and does not stand in the truth, because there is no truth in him. Whenever he tells a lie he speaks from his heart, because he is a liar and the father of the same. ⁴⁵ Yet, because *I* tell the truth you don't believe Me. ⁴⁶ Which of you convicts Me of sin? But if I do tell the truth, why don't you believe Me? ⁴⁷ Anyone who belongs to God listens to God's words. That's why you don't listen, because you don't belong to God."

BEFORE ABRAHAM WAS, I AM

⁴⁸ So in reply the Jews said to Him,

"Aren't we right in saying You are a Samaritan and have a demon?"

⁴⁹ "I do not have a demon," Jesus answered. "On the contrary, I honor My Father, and you dishonor Me. ⁵⁰ Yet I do not seek My glory; there is One who is seeking it, and He is the Judge.

⁵¹ "Amen, amen,* I tell you, if anyone keeps My word he will never see death."

⁵² Then the Jews said to Him,

"Now we know You have a demon! Abraham died and so did the prophets; yet *You* say, 'If anyone keeps My word he will never taste death'? [53] Surely You aren't greater than our father Abraham, who died? The prophets also died. Who do You make Yourself out to be?"

[54] "If I honor Myself," Jesus answered, "My honor is nothing. It is My Father who honors Me, of whom *you* say, 'He is our God.' [55] Yet you have not known Him, but I do know Him. And if I were to say I don't know Him, I would be a liar like you. But I do know Him and I keep His word. [56] Your father Abraham was overjoyed to see My day, and he saw it and was glad."

[57] Then the Jews said to Him,

"You aren't fifty years old yet, and have You seen Abraham?"

[58] Jesus said to them,

"Amen, amen, I tell you, before Abraham was, I AM!"

[59] Therefore they picked up stones to throw at Him. But Jesus hid Himself and went out of the temple courts, going through the midst of them, and so passed by.

JESUS HEALS A MAN BORN BLIND

9 Now as He was passing by He saw a man who had been blind from birth. [2] And His disciples questioned Him, saying,

"Rabbi, who sinned, this man or his parents, that he was born blind?"

[3] "Neither this man sinned nor his parents," Jesus replied. "But this came about so that God's works might be displayed in him. [4] I must do the works of the One who sent Me while it is day. Night is coming when nobody can work. [5] As long as I am in the world, I am the Light of the world."

[6] After He said these things He spat on the ground, made clay from the saliva, and spread the clay on the blind man's eyes. [7] "Go," He told him, "wash in the pool of Siloam" (which means Sent). So he went and washed, and came back seeing.

[8] Then the neighbors and those who had seen him formerly, that he was blind, said, "Isn't this the man who sat begging?"

[9] Others were saying,

"He's the one."

But still others were saying,

"He looks like him."

He kept saying,

"I'm the one!"

¹⁰ Therefore they said to him,

"How did it happen that your eyes were opened?"

¹¹ He answered and said,

"A man named Jesus made clay, spread it on my eyes, and told me, 'Go to the pool of Siloam and wash.' So when I went and washed I received my sight!"

¹² Then they said to him,

"Where is He?"

"I don't know," he replied.

THE PHARISEES EXCOMMUNICATE THE HEALED MAN

¹³ They brought the man who was formerly blind to the Pharisees. ¹⁴ Now it was a Sabbath when Jesus made clay and opened his eyes. ¹⁵ So once again the Pharisees also asked him how he received his sight.

"He put clay on my eyes," he told them; "I washed and I see."

¹⁶ Therefore some of the Pharisees said,

"This man is not from God, because He doesn't keep the Sabbath."

Others were saying,

"How can a sinful man perform such miraculous signs?" And there was a division among them.

¹⁷ They said to the man again,

"What do *you* say about Him, since He has opened your eyes?"

So he said,

"He's a prophet."

¹⁸ But the Jews did not believe concerning him—that he was blind and received sight—until they summoned the parents of the one who had received his sight.

¹⁹ Then they asked them,

"Is this your son, whom *you* say was born blind? So how is it that he can now see?"

[20] And his parents answered them,

"We know this is our son and that he was born blind. [21] But how it is that he can now see we don't know, and who opened his eyes we don't know. He is of age; ask him." [22] His parents said these things because they were afraid of the Jews, for the leaders had already decided that if anyone confessed Him to be the Christ, he would be barred from the synagogue. [23] For this reason his parents said, "He is of age; ask him." [24] So a second time they summoned the man who had been blind and told him,

"Give glory to God. *We* know that this man is a sinner!"

[25] So he answered,

"Whether or not He's a sinner, I don't know. One thing I do know: though I was blind, now I see!"

[26] Then they asked him again,

"What did He do to you? How did He open your eyes?"

[27] "I already told you," he answered them, "and you didn't listen. Why do you want to hear it again? *You* don't want to become His disciples too, do you?"

[28] They reviled him, saying,

"*You* are that fellow's disciple, but *we* are *Moses'* disciples. [29] *We* know that God has spoken to Moses. But this fellow—we don't know where He's from!"

[30] "This is a remarkable thing," the man answered them. "You don't know where He is from and yet He opened my eyes! [31] And we know that God doesn't listen to sinners; but if anyone is God-fearing and does His will, He listens to him. [32] Since time began it has been unheard of that anyone opened the eyes of a person born blind! [33] If this man were not from God He wouldn't be able to do anything."

[34] In reply they told him,

"You were totally born in sin—and are you trying to teach us?" So they threw him out.

THE BLIND MAN'S SIGHT
AND THE PHARISEES' BLINDNESS

[35] Jesus heard that they had thrown him out. And when He found him He asked him,

"Do you believe in the Son of God?"*

³⁶ Replying, he said,

"And who is He, Sir, that I may believe in Him?"

³⁷ Then Jesus said to him,

"You have both seen Him and He is the One who is speaking with you."

³⁸ So he said,

"Lord, I believe!" And he worshiped Him.

³⁹ "I came into this world for judgment," Jesus said, "so that those who do not see may see and that those who do see may become blind."

⁴⁰ And some of the Pharisees who were with Him heard these things, and asked Him,

"We aren't blind, too, are we?"

⁴¹ "If you were blind," Jesus told them, "you wouldn't have sin. But now you say, 'We see!' Therefore your sin remains."

The Ideal Shepherd

10 "Amen, amen,* I tell you, anyone who doesn't enter the sheepfold by the door, but climbs up some other way, he is a thief and a robber. ² But the one who enters by the door is the shepherd of the sheep. ³ To him the doorkeeper opens, and the sheep hear his voice; he calls his own sheep by name and leads them out. ⁴ And when he has brought his own sheep outside he goes ahead of them, and the sheep follow him because they know his voice. ⁵ But they will *not* follow a stranger; on the contrary they will run away from him, because they don't know the voice of strangers."

⁶ Jesus gave them this illustration, but they didn't understand what He was telling them.

The Good Shepherd

⁷ So Jesus said to them again,

"Amen, amen, I tell you, I am the door of the sheep. ⁸ All who came before Me are thieves and robbers, but the sheep didn't listen to them. ⁹ I am the door. If anyone enters *by Me*, he will be saved, and will come in and go out and find pasture. ¹⁰ A thief comes only to steal, and to kill, and to destroy. I have come that they may have life and that they may have it in abundance.

[11] "I am the good shepherd. The good shepherd lays down his life for the sheep. [12] But the hired man, who is not the shepherd and does not own the sheep, seeing a wolf coming, leaves the sheep and runs away. Then the wolf snatches the sheep and scatters them. [13] And the hired man flees because he *is* a hired man and doesn't care about the sheep. [14] I am the good shepherd, and I know My own sheep, and I am known by My own. [15] Just as the Father knows Me, I also know the Father, and I lay down My life for the sheep. [16] I have other sheep, too, which do not belong to this fold. I must bring *them* also, and they will listen to My voice. Then there will be one flock, one shepherd. [17] For this reason the Father loves Me, because I am laying down My life in order to take it up again. [18] No one takes it from Me, but I lay it down of My own accord. I have the authority to lay it down and I have the authority to take it up again. This command I have received from My Father."

[19] Therefore a division took place among the Jews, because of these words. [20] And many of them were saying,

"He has a demon and He's crazy! Why do you listen to Him?"

[21] But others were saying,

"These aren't the words of someone who has a demon. A demon can't open blind people's eyes, can he?"

JESUS AT THE FESTIVAL OF HANNUKAH

[22] Now it was the festival of Dedication in Jerusalem; and it was winter. [23] Jesus was walking in the temple courts in Solomon's Colonnade. [24] So the Jews surrounded Him and said to Him,

"How long are you going to keep us in suspense? If You are the Christ, tell us plainly."

[25] "I did tell you and you don't believe," Jesus answered them. "The works that I do in My Father's name—these testify about Me. [26] But *you* don't believe, since you don't belong to My sheep, just as I told you. [27] My sheep hear My voice, and I know them, and they follow Me. [28] And I give them eternal life, and they will never, ever perish, and no one will snatch them out of My hand. [29] My Father, who has given them to Me, is greater than all; and no

one is able to snatch them out of My Father's hand. ³⁰ I and the Father are one."

RENEWED EFFORTS TO STONE JESUS

³¹ Therefore the Jews picked up stones again to stone Him.

³² "I have shown you many good works from My Father," Jesus answered them. "For which one of these works are you stoning Me?"

³³ The Jews answered Him, saying,

"We are not stoning You for a good work, but for blasphemy, and because You, being a man, make Yourself God."

³⁴ Jesus answered them,

"Isn't it written in your law, *'I said, you are gods'?* ³⁵ If He called them 'gods' to whom the Word of God came—and Scripture cannot be broken— ³⁶ do you say 'You are blaspheming' to the One the Father set apart and sent into the world, because I said 'I am the Son of God'? ³⁷ If I am not doing My Father's works, don't believe Me. ³⁸ But if I am doing them, even if you don't believe Me, believe the works, so that you may know and believe that the Father is in Me and I in Him."

³⁹ Therefore they were trying again to seize Him, but He eluded their grasp.

MANY BEYOND THE JORDAN RIVER BELIEVE IN JESUS

⁴⁰ So He went back across the Jordan to the place where John was baptizing at first, and He remained there. ⁴¹ Then many came to Him and said,

"John didn't perform a single miraculous sign, but everything John said about this man was true." ⁴² And many believed in Him there.

LAZARUS DIES AT BETHANY

11 Now a certain man, Lazarus of Bethany, the village of Mary and her sister Martha, was sick. ² This was the Mary who anointed the Lord with fragrant oil and wiped His feet with her hair, whose brother Lazarus was sick. ³ So the sisters sent word to Him, saying,

"Lord, the one You love is sick."

[4] When Jesus heard it, He said,

"This sickness will not end in death, but is for the glory of God, so that the Son of God may be glorified through it." [5] Now Jesus loved Martha and her sister and Lazarus. [6] So, when He heard that he was sick, He stayed two more days in the place where He was. [7] Then, after this, He said to the disciples,

"Let's go to Judea again."

[8] "Rabbi," the disciples told Him, "the Judeans were just now trying to stone You, and are You going there again?"

[9] Jesus answered,

"Aren't there 12 hours in a day? If anyone walks during the day he doesn't stumble, because he sees the light of this world. [10] But if anyone walks during the night he does stumble, because the light is not in him." [11] He said these things, and after that He told them, "Our friend Lazarus has fallen asleep, but I am on My way to wake him up."

[12] Then His disciples said,

"Lord, if he has fallen asleep he will get well." [13] Jesus, however, had been speaking of his death, but they thought He was speaking about natural sleep. [14] So Jesus then told them plainly,

"Lazarus has died, [15] and I'm glad for your sakes that I wasn't there, so that you may believe. But let's go to him."

[16] Then Thomas (called Twin) said to his fellow disciples,

"Let *us* go too, so that we may die with Him."

THE RESURRECTION AND THE LIFE

[17] So when Jesus came, He found that Lazarus had already been in the tomb four days. [18] Now Bethany was near Jerusalem, about two miles away. [19] And many of the Jews had come to the women around Martha and Mary, in order to comfort them about their brother. [20] So, as soon as Martha heard that Jesus was coming, she went to meet Him; but Mary remained sitting in the house. [21] Then Martha said to Jesus,

"Lord, if You had been here, my brother wouldn't have died. [22] But even now I know that God will give You whatever You ask God for."

²³ "Your brother will rise again," Jesus told her.

²⁴ Martha said to Him,

"I know that he will rise again in the resurrection at the last day."

²⁵ Jesus said to her,

"I am the Resurrection and the Life. He who believes in Me, even if he dies, will live. ²⁶ And everyone who lives and believes in Me will never die. Do you believe this?"

²⁷ "Yes, Lord," she told Him, "I believe that You are the Christ, the Son of God, who was to come into the world."

JESUS SHARES THE SORROW OF DEATH

²⁸ And when she had said these things, she went back and called her sister Mary privately, saying,

"The Teacher is here and is calling for you!" ²⁹ As soon as she heard this, she got up quickly and went to Him. ³⁰ Now Jesus had not yet come into the village, but was in the place where Martha had met Him. ³¹ So when the Jews who were with her in the house, consoling her, saw that Mary got up quickly and went out, they followed her, saying,

"She's going to the tomb to weep there." ³² So when Mary came where Jesus was and saw Him, she fell down at His feet and told Him,

"Lord, if You had been here, my brother wouldn't have died!"

³³ So when Jesus saw her crying, and the Jews who had come with her crying, He groaned in His spirit and was deeply moved. ³⁴ And He said,

"Where have you put him?"

John 11:25-27. This is one of the most comforting passages in the Bible. It is often read at funerals because it is Jesus' guarantee that eternal life belongs to everyone who believes in Him.

He presents Himself as the long-awaited Christ, man's Savior (verse 27), who came into the world bringing resurrection and eternal life to those who believe in Him. He then elaborates. This means, Jesus tells Martha, that even if a believer dies he or she will be resurrected and live forever.

Jesus says to Martha, "Do you believe this?" Dear reader, do *you* believe this? If you do, Jesus guarantees that you have eternal life and even if you should die, you will be resurrected from the dead to live with Him forever.

"Lord," they told Him, "come and see."

³⁵ Jesus shed tears.

³⁶ So the Jews said,

"See how He loved him!"

³⁷ But some of them said,

"Couldn't He who opened the blind man's eyes have also kept this man from dying?"

JESUS RAISES LAZARUS FROM THE DEAD

³⁸ Then Jesus, groaning in Himself again, came to the tomb. Now it was a cave, and a stone was lying against it.

³⁹ "Take away the stone," Jesus said.

Martha, the dead man's sister, told Him,

"Lord, by now there is a stench, because he's been in the tomb four days."

⁴⁰ Jesus said to her,

"Didn't I tell you that if you believed you would see the glory of God?"

⁴¹ So they took away the stone from where the dead man was lying. Then Jesus raised His eyes and said,

"Father, I thank You that You heard Me. ⁴² Yet *I* know that You always hear Me, but for the sake of the crowd standing around I said this, so that they may believe that You sent Me." ⁴³ And after saying these things He shouted with a loud voice, "Lazarus, come out!" ⁴⁴ So the dead man came out bound hand and foot with linen strips, and his face wrapped with a handkerchief. Jesus said to them, "Loose him and let him go."

THE PLOT TO KILL JESUS

⁴⁵ Therefore many of the Jews who came to Mary and saw the things Jesus did, believed in Him. ⁴⁶ But some of them went off to the Pharisees and told them the things Jesus did. ⁴⁷ Then the chief priests and the Pharisees convened the Sanhedrin and said,

"What are we going to do? For this man performs many miraculous signs. ⁴⁸ If we let Him alone like this, everybody will believe in Him! Then the Romans will come and blot out both our Place and our Nation."

⁴⁹ But one of them, Caiaphas, who was high priest that year, said to them,

"You know nothing at all! ⁵⁰ Nor are you considering that it is to our advantage that one man should die for the people, and not that the whole nation should perish." ⁵¹ Now he did not say this of his own accord; but being high priest that year he prophesied that Jesus was going to die for the nation, ⁵² and not only for the nation, but also in order to unite the scattered children of God. ⁵³ So from that day on they plotted to kill Him. ⁵⁴ Therefore Jesus no longer walked openly among the Judeans, but went from there to the region near the desert, to a town called Ephraim. And He spent time there with His disciples.

⁵⁵ Now the Jewish Passover was near, and before the Passover many went up to Jerusalem from the country to purify themselves. ⁵⁶ Then they were looking for Jesus and asking one another as they stood in the temple courts:

"What do you think—that He won't come to the festival at all?"

⁵⁷ Now both the chief priests and the Pharisees had given an order that if anyone knew where He was he should report it, so they could arrest Him.

THE ANOINTING AT BETHANY

12 Then Jesus, six days before the Passover, came to Bethany. Lazarus, who had died—the one He had raised from the dead—was there. ² So they gave a dinner for Him there, and Martha waited on them. Now Lazarus was one of those reclining at the table with Him. ³ Then Mary took a pound of pure and expensive oil of nard, anointed Jesus' feet, and wiped His feet with her hair. So the house was filled with the fragrance of the oil.

⁴ Then one of His disciples, Judas Iscariot, Simon's son (who was about to betray Him) said,

⁵ "Why wasn't this fragrant oil sold for 300 denarii and given to the poor?" ⁶ However, he didn't say this because he cared about the poor but because he was a thief, was in charge of the money-box, and used to help himself to what was put into it.

⁷ Then Jesus said,

"Leave her alone. She has kept this for the day of My burial. [8] For you always have the poor with you, but you do not always have Me."

THE PLOT TO KILL LAZARUS

[9] Then a large crowd of the Jews learned that He was there. They came not only because of Jesus, but also to see Lazarus, whom He had raised from the dead. [10] However, the chief priests decided to kill Lazarus too, [11] because he was the reason many of the Jews were falling away and believing in Jesus.

THE TRIUMPHAL ENTRY

[12] The next day a large crowd that had come to the festival, when they heard that Jesus was coming to Jerusalem, [13] took palm branches and went out to meet Him. And they shouted,

"'Hosanna!
'Blessed is He who comes in the Name of the Lord,'
The King of Israel!"

[14] Now Jesus found a young donkey and mounted it, just as it is written,

[15] *"Fear no more, Daughter of Zion;*
See, your King is coming,
Sitting on a donkey's colt!"

[16] Yet His disciples did not understand these things at first. However, when Jesus was glorified, then they remembered that these things had been written about Him and that they had done these things to Him. [17] So the crowd that had been with Him when He called Lazarus out of the tomb and raised him from the dead continued to testify. [18] That is also why the crowd met Him, because they heard that He had performed this miraculous sign. [19] Then the Pharisees said to one another,

"You see that you're accomplishing absolutely nothing! Look, the world has gone after Him!"

GREEKS SEEKING JESUS

[20] Now there were some Greeks among those who went up to worship at the festival. [21] So these men came to Philip, who was from Bethsaida in Galilee, and made this request of him:

"Sir, we want to see Jesus."

²² Philip went and told Andrew, and then Andrew and Philip told Jesus. ²³ But Jesus answered them,

"The hour has come for the Son of Man to be glorified.

²⁴ "Amen, amen,* I tell you, unless a grain of wheat falls into the ground and dies, it remains by itself. But if it dies, it produces a large crop. ²⁵ Whoever loves his life will lose it, and whoever hates his life in this world will keep it for eternal life. ²⁶ If anyone serves Me, let him follow Me. And where *I* am, there My servant will be also. And if anyone serves Me, the Father will honor him.

JESUS PREDICTS HIS CRUCIFIXION

²⁷ "Now My soul is distressed, and what shall I say—'Father, save Me from this hour'? But for this reason I came to this hour. ²⁸ Father, glorify Your Name!"

Then a voice came from heaven:

"I have both glorified it and I will glorify it again!"

²⁹ So the crowd which stood by and heard it said that it had thundered. Others said,

"An angel has spoken to Him!"

³⁰ Jesus responded,

"It was not because of Me that this voice came, but for your sakes. ³¹ Now is the judgment of this world. Now the ruler of this world will be cast out. ³² And as for Me, if I am lifted up from the earth I will draw all peoples to Myself." ³³ Now He said this to indicate what kind of death He was about to die.

³⁴ The crowd answered Him,

"*We* have heard from the Law that the Christ remains forever. So how can *You* say, 'The Son of Man must be lifted up'? Who is this Son of Man?"

³⁵ Then Jesus said to them,

"The light will be with you a little while longer. Walk while you have the light, so that the darkness doesn't overtake you. The one who walks in darkness doesn't know where he is going. ³⁶ While you have the light believe in the light, so that you may become sons of light."

ISAIAH'S PROPHECY FULFILLED

Jesus spoke these things, and went away and hid from them. ³⁷ But though He had performed so many miraculous signs in their presence, they did not believe in Him. ³⁸ This was to fulfill the word of Isaiah the prophet, which He spoke:

"Lord, who has believed our report?
And to whom has the arm of the Lord been revealed?"

³⁹ The reason they were unable to believe is because Isaiah said again:

⁴⁰*"He has blinded their eyes*
And hardened their hearts,
So that they would not see with their eyes
Nor understand with their hearts,
And be converted,
And I would heal them."

⁴¹ Isaiah said these things when he saw His glory and spoke about Him.

⁴² Nevertheless, even among the rulers many believed in Him, but because of the Pharisees they did not confess Him, so they wouldn't be barred from the synagogue. ⁴³ For they loved praise from men more than praise from God.

DARKNESS AND LIGHT

⁴⁴ But Jesus cried out and said,

"Whoever believes in Me, believes not in Me, but in Him who sent Me. ⁴⁵ And whoever sees Me sees Him who sent Me. ⁴⁶ I have come as a light into the world, so that no one who believes in Me would remain in darkness. ⁴⁷ And if someone hears My words and doesn't believe, *I* don't judge him; because I didn't come to judge the world but to save the world. ⁴⁸ Whoever rejects Me and doesn't accept My sayings has his judge: the word which I have spoken will judge him on the Last Day. ⁴⁹ For I have not spoken on My own authority, but the Father who sent Me, He gave Me a command, what I should say and what I should speak. ⁵⁰ And I know that His command is eternal life. So the things which I speak, just as the Father has told Me, so I speak."

Jesus Washes His Disciples' Feet

13 Now before the Passover festival, since Jesus knew that His hour had come to depart from this world to the Father, having loved His own who were in the world He loved them to the end.

² And when supper was served, the devil already having put it into the heart of Judas Iscariot, Simon's son, to betray Him, ³ since Jesus knew that the Father had given everything into His hands, and that He had come forth from God and was going back to God, ⁴ He got up from supper and laid aside His robe. Then He took a towel and tied it around Himself. ⁵ Next He poured water into a basin and began to wash His disciples' feet and to dry them with the towel which was tied around Him. ⁶ So He came to Simon Peter, who said to Him,

"Lord, do *You* wash *my* feet?"

⁷ In reply Jesus said to him,

"What I'm doing you don't understand now, but afterward you will."

⁸ "You shall never wash my feet," Peter told Him, "not ever!" Jesus answered him,

"If I don't wash you, you have no part with Me."

⁹ Simon Peter said to Him,

"Lord, not only my feet, but also my hands and my head!"

¹⁰ Jesus told him,

"One who is bathed has no need except to wash his feet, but he is wholly clean. And *you* are clean, but not all of you." ¹¹ For He knew who would betray Him. Therefore He said, "You are not *all* clean."

The Meaning of Footwashing

¹² So when Jesus had washed their feet and put His robe back on, He reclined again and said to them,

"Do you know what I have done to you? ¹³ *You* call Me Teacher and Lord, and you speak rightly, since I am. ¹⁴ So if I, your Lord and Teacher, have washed your feet, *you* also ought to wash one another's feet. ¹⁵ In fact, I have given you an example, that *you* also should do just as I have done to you.

¹⁶"Amen, amen,* I tell you, a slave is not greater than his master, nor is a messenger greater than the one who sent him. ¹⁷ If you know these things, you are blest if you do them! ¹⁸ I'm not talking about all of you. I know those I've chosen. But let the Scripture be fulfilled:

'The one who eats bread with Me
Has kicked his heel at Me.'

¹⁹ "I'm telling you *now* before it happens, so that when it does happen you will believe that I am He.

²⁰ "Amen, amen, I tell you, whoever receives anyone I send receives Me, and whoever receives Me receives Him who sent Me."

JUDAS'S BETRAYAL PREDICTED

²¹ When Jesus had said these things He was distressed in spirit and testified, saying,

"Amen, amen, I tell you, one of you will betray Me!"

²² Then the disciples looked at one another, at a loss as to whom He was talking about.

²³ Now one of His disciples, whom Jesus loved, was leaning back against the front of Jesus' robe. ²⁴ So Simon Peter motioned to him to find out who it was He was talking about. ²⁵ And he leaned back against Jesus' heart and said to Him,

"Lord, who is it?"

²⁶ Jesus answered,

"It is the one I hand the bit of bread to after I've dipped it." And when He had dipped the bread He gave it to Judas Iscariot, Simon's son. ²⁷ So after the bread Satan entered into him. Therefore Jesus told him,

"What you're doing, do quickly!"

²⁸ But none of those reclining at the table knew why He told him this. ²⁹ Since Judas had the moneybox, some in fact thought that Jesus was telling him, "Buy what we need for the festival," or that he should give something to the poor. ³⁰ So when he had received the bread, he went out immediately.

And it was night.

THE NEW COMMANDMENT

³¹ After he went out Jesus said,

"Now the Son of Man is glorified, and God is glorified in Him. ³² If God is glorified in Him, God will also glorify Him in Himself, and will glorify Him at once.

³³ "Little children, I am with you a little while longer. You will look for Me, and just as I told the Judeans, 'Where I am going you cannot come,' so now I tell you.

³⁴ "I give you a new commandment, that you love one another just as I have loved you, that you also love one another. ³⁵ By this all people will know that you are My disciples, if you have love for one another."

PETER'S DENIAL PREDICTED

³⁶ "Lord," Simon Peter said to Him, "where are You going?"

Jesus answered him,

"Where I am going you cannot follow Me now; but you will follow Me later."

³⁷ "Lord," Peter asked Him, "why can't I follow You now? I will lay down my life for You!"

³⁸ Jesus answered him,

"Will you lay down your life for Me? Amen, amen,* I tell you, the rooster will not crow till you have denied Me three times!

John 13:31-17:26. This large section of John's Gospel is often referred to as the Upper Room Discourse. Here the Lord gave final instructions to His eleven faithful disciples, offered them the closest relationship possible with Himself, and prayed for them and all believers of all time who would follow Him.

Friendship with the Son of God is an important secondary theme of this book. Although eternal life is presented as a gift freely given to every believer (John 3:16), a *close* personal relationship is offered only to those who abide in His love by obeying His commands.

If you have received eternal life by believing in Christ (John 5:24) and you desire this friendship that Jesus offers, read these four chapters carefully. You can know the joy and fruitfulness that close friendship with your Savior brings when you respond to His invitation to live in His love by doing what He says.

JESUS IS THE WAY, THE TRUTH, AND THE LIFE

14 "Do not let your heart be distressed. Believe in God, believe also in Me. ² In My Father's house are many homes, otherwise I would have told you. I am going away to prepare a place for you. ³ And if I go away and prepare a place for you, I will come back and receive you to Myself, so that where *I* am *you* may be also. ⁴ And where I am going you know, and you know the way."

⁵ "Lord," Thomas said to Him, "we don't know where You're going, and how can we know the way?"

⁶ Jesus told him,

"*I* am the Way and the Truth and the Life. No one comes to the Father except through Me.

JESUS REVEALS THE FATHER

⁷ "If you had known Me, you would have known My Father too. And from now on you do know Him and have seen Him."

⁸ "Lord," Philip said to Him, "show us the Father, and that's enough for us."

⁹ Jesus answered him,

"Have I been with you all this time, and you haven't known Me, Philip? The one who has seen Me has seen the Father. So how can you say, 'Show us the Father'? ¹⁰ Don't you believe that I am in the Father and the Father is in Me? The words I speak to you I do not speak on My own authority. But it is the Father who dwells in Me who does the works. ¹¹ Believe Me that I am in the Father and the Father is in Me. Otherwise, believe Me because of the works themselves.

IN JESUS' NAME

¹² "Amen, amen,* I tell you, the one who believes in Me will also do the works that I do, and will do greater works than these, because I am going to My Father. ¹³ And whatever you ask in My Name, I will do it, so that the Father may be glorified in the Son.

[14] If you ask anything in My Name, I will do it. [15] If you love Me, keep* My commandments.

ANOTHER ADVOCATE PROMISED

[16] "Also I will ask the Father, and He will give you another Advocate, so that He may stay with you forever. [17] He is the Spirit of truth, whom the world is unable to receive because it doesn't see Him or know Him. You do know Him, however, because He stays with you and will be in you. [18] I won't leave you as orphans; I am coming to you.

THE FATHER, THE SON, AND THE HOLY SPIRIT

[19] "In a little while the world will see Me no longer. You, however, will see Me. Because I live, you will live too. [20] In that day you will know that I am in My Father, you are in Me, and I in you. [21] The one who has My commandments and keeps them is the one who loves Me. And the one who loves Me will be loved by My Father. I will love him too and reveal Myself to him."

[22] Judas (not Iscariot) said to him,

"Lord, so how is it You're going to reveal Yourself to *us* and not to the world?"

[23] In reply Jesus said to him,

"If anyone loves Me he will keep My word. My Father will love him too, and We will come to him and make Our home with him. [24] The one who doesn't love Me doesn't keep My words. Yet the word which you heard is not Mine but the Father's who sent Me.

[25] "These things I have spoken to you while I am still with you. [26] But the Advocate, the Holy Spirit, whom the Father will send in My Name, is the One who will teach you all things and remind you of all the things I have told you.

John 14:15. The primary motivation for the obedience which draws believers into a close friendship with their Savior is love. Those who become Christ's friends are those believers who do what He says because they love Him.

Dear reader, when you obey Jesus you demonstrate your love for Him. Jesus has a special affection for obedient believers. And since there are no secrets between friends, Christ promises that He will not withhold any truth from them (verse 21).

JESUS' GIFT OF PEACE

[27] "Peace I leave with you. *My* peace I give to you. I don't give to you as the world gives. Do not let your heart be distressed or intimidated. [28] You have heard that I told you, 'I am going away and I am coming to you.' If you loved Me you would have been glad that I said, 'I am going to the Father,' because My Father is greater than I. [29] And now I have told you before it happens, so that when it does happen, you may believe. [30] I will no longer talk much with you, because the ruler of this world is coming, and he has nothing in Me! [31] On the contrary, so that the world may know that I love the Father, and just as the Father commanded Me, so I do.

"Get up, let's leave this place.

THE FRUITFUL LIFE IN CHRIST

15 "I am the true vine and My Father is the vinedresser. [2] Every branch in Me which does not produce fruit He props up, and every one producing fruit He prunes so that it will produce more fruit. [3] *You* are already clean because of the word I have spoken to you. [4] Abide in Me, and I in you. Just as a branch is unable to produce fruit by itself, unless it abides in the vine, so neither can you unless you abide in Me.

[5] "I am the vine, you are the branches. The one who abides in Me, and I in him, is the one who produces much fruit, since you can do nothing apart from Me. [6] If anyone does not abide in Me, he is thrown aside like a branch and withers. Then they gather such branches, throw them into the fire, and they are burned. [7] If you abide in Me and My words abide in you, you will ask whatever you wish, and it shall be done for you. [8] My Father is glorified by this: that you produce much fruit. So you will be My disciples.

CHRISTLIKE LOVE

[9] "Just as the Father has loved Me, I also have loved you. Abide in My love. [10] If you keep My commandments, you will abide in My love, just as I have kept My Father's commandments and abide in His love.

¹¹ "I have spoken these things to you so that My joy may abide in you and your joy may be complete. ¹² This is My commandment, that you love one another just as I have loved you. ¹³ Greater love has no one than this, that someone would lay down his life for his friends. ¹⁴ *You* are My friends if you do whatever I command you. ¹⁵ I don't call you *servants* any more, because a servant doesn't know what his master is doing. But I have called you *friends*, because I have made known to you everything I have heard from My Father. ¹⁶ You did not choose Me, but I chose you and appointed you that you should go out and produce much fruit, and that your fruit should endure, so that whatever you ask the Father in My Name, He will give you. ¹⁷ These things I command you: that you love one another.

PERSECUTIONS PREDICTED

¹⁸ "If the world hates you, be sure that it hated Me before it hated you. ¹⁹ If you were of the world, the world would love its own. Yet, because you are not of the world, but I have chosen you out of the world, the world hates you. ²⁰ Keep in mind the statement that I made to you: 'A servant is not greater than his master.' If they persecuted Me, they will also persecute you. If they kept My word, they will also keep yours. ²¹ On the contrary, they will do all these things to you for My Name's sake, because they don't know the One who sent Me. ²² If I hadn't come and spoken to them, they would have no sin. But now they have no excuse for their sin. ²³ The one who hates Me hates My Father too. ²⁴ If I hadn't done the works among them which no one else has done, they would have no sin. But now they have seen and hated both

---

John 15:14-17. This is the clearest and simplest expression of both the terms for friendship and the definition of this special relationship with Jesus Christ.

The terms for becoming Jesus' friend are very clear. Faith in Jesus brings eternal life (John 6:47), but only those believers who obey His commands will experience a *close* personal relationship with the Son of God (15:14).

The definition of friendship with the Son of God is: A relationship in which the Lord fully discloses His thoughts (15:15-17). This means He helps us to understand His Word, the Bible.

Me and My Father. [25] But this is so that the statement written in their law might be fulfilled:

'They hated me for no reason.'

COMING TESTIMONY AND REJECTION

[26] "However, when the Advocate comes, whom I will send to you from the Father, the Spirit of truth who proceeds from the Father, He will testify concerning Me. [27] And you also will testify, because you have been with Me from the beginning.

16 "I have spoken these things to you to keep you from stumbling [2] They will bar you from the synagogues. In fact, a time is coming when anyone who kills you will think he is offering service to God! [3] And they will do these things because they haven't known the Father or Me. [4] But I have told you these things so that when the time comes you may remember that I told them to you. Yet I didn't tell you these things from the beginning, because I was with you.

THE ADVOCATE'S MINISTRY

[5] "However, now I am going away to Him who sent Me, but not one of you asks Me, 'Where are you going?' [6] Yet, because I have spoken these things to you, sorrow has filled your heart. [7] Nevertheless I am telling you the truth. It is beneficial for you that I do go away, because if I don't go away the Advocate will not come to you. But if I do go, I will send Him to you. [8] And when He comes He will convict the world concerning sin and righteousness and judgment: [9] concerning sin, because they don't believe in Me; [10] concerning righteousness, because I am going away to My Father and you will no longer see Me; [11] and concerning judgment, because the ruler of this world has been judged.

[12] "I still have many things to tell you, but you can't bear them now. [13] But when He, the Spirit of truth, comes, He will guide you into all the truth. For He will not speak on His own authority, but He will speak whatever He hears. He will also declare to you the things that are to come. [14] He will glorify Me, because He will take from what is Mine and declare it to you. [15] Everything that the Father has is Mine. That is why I told you that He takes from what is Mine and will communicate it to you.

SORROW TURNED TO JOY

¹⁶ "A little while and you will not see Me; and again a little while and you will see Me, because I am going to the Father."

¹⁷ Then some of His disciples said to one another,

"What is this that He tells us: 'A little while and you will not see Me; and again a little while and you will see Me'; and, 'because I am going to the Father'?" ¹⁸ So they said, "What is this that He says, 'A little while'? We don't know what He's talking about!"

¹⁹ Therefore Jesus knew they wanted to question Him and said to them,

"Are you discussing among yourselves what I said, 'A little while and you will not see Me; and again a little while and you will see Me'?

²⁰ "Amen, amen,* I tell you, you will weep and wail, but the world will be glad; you will become sorrowful, but your sorrow will turn to joy. ²¹ When a woman is in labor she has pain because her time has come. But when she has given birth to the baby, she no longer remembers the anguish, for joy that a human being has been born into the world. ²² Therefore you also have sorrow now. But I will see you again; then your heart will be joyful and no one will rob you of your joy. ²³ In that day you will ask Me nothing.

"Amen, amen, I tell you, whatever you ask the Father in My name He will give you. ²⁴ Until now you have asked for nothing in My name. Ask and you will receive, that your joy may be complete.

CHRIST THE VICTOR

²⁵ "These things I have spoken to you in figurative language. But a time is coming when I will no longer speak to you in figurative language, but I will tell you plainly about the Father. ²⁶ In that day you will pray in My Name. Yet I'm not telling you that I will make request to the Father on your behalf. ²⁷ For the Father Himself loves you, because you have loved Me and you have believed that I came forth from God. ²⁸ I did come forth from the Father and I have come into the world. Again, I am leaving the world and going to the Father."

²⁹ "Ah," His disciples told Him, "now You're speaking plainly, and using no figurative language! ³⁰ Now we know that You know

everything and don't need anyone to question You. By this we believe that You came forth from God."

³¹ Jesus answered them,

"Do you now believe? ³² Listen: The time is coming, and has now come, when you will be scattered each to his own home, and you will leave Me alone. Yet I am not alone, because the Father is with Me. ³³ I have told you these things so that in Me you may have peace. In the world you have tribulation. But take heart! I have conquered the world."

JESUS PRAYS FOR HIMSELF

17 Jesus spoke these things, raised His eyes to Heaven, and said:

"Father, the hour has come!
Glorify Your Son, so that Your Son also
may glorify You,
² just as You gave Him authority over all humanity,
so that He will give eternal life to all whom You
have given Him.
³ And this is eternal life, that they may know You,
the only true God, and the One whom You have
sent—Jesus Christ.
⁴ I have glorified You on the earth.
I have completed the work You have given Me
to do.
⁵ And now, Father, glorify Me at Your side
with the glory which I had at Your side
before the world existed.

John 16:33. One of the major themes of this section on friendship with the Lord (see note at 13:31) is the warning that Jesus' friends will make enemies of the world (15:18–16:15). Persecution is the likely result of a close personal relationship with the Son of God. But friends of Jesus should not be discouraged by this news. A corresponding and more pronounced theme is Jesus' promise of peace in the midst of suffering (16:16-33). Peace comes to the friend of Christ who trusts in Jesus' assuring words that, in spite of opposition, "I have conquered the world."

Jesus Prays For His Disciples

⁶"I have revealed Your Name to the men whom
   You have given Me out of the world;
   they were Yours, you have given them to Me,
   and they have kept Your word.

⁷ Now they have come to know that all things
   You have given to Me are from You.

⁸ For the words which You have given to Me, I have
   given to them; and they have received them
   and known for sure that I came forth from You.
   And they have believed that You sent Me.

⁹ I pray for them. I am not praying for the world,
   but for those whom You have given Me,
   because they are Yours.

¹⁰ And all My things are Yours, and Yours are Mine,
   and I have been glorified in them.

¹¹ Now I am no longer in the world, but these are in
   the world, and I am coming to You.

"Holy Father, protect them through Your Name
   which You have given to Me,
   so that they may be one just as We are.

¹² While I was with them in the world I protected
   them through Your Name. Those whom You have
   given Me I guarded; and not one of them is lost
   except the son of perdition,
   that the Scripture may be fulfilled.

¹³ But now I am coming to You, and I speak
   these things in the world so that they may have
   My joy fulfilled in them.

¹⁴ I have given them Your word; and the world hated
   them because they are not of the world,
   just as I am not of the world.

¹⁵ I am not praying that You take them out of the
   world, but that You protect them
   from the Evil One.

[16] They are not of the world,
just as I am not of the world.
[17] Sanctify them by Your truth; Your word is truth.
[18] Just as You sent Me into the world,
I also have sent them into the world.
[19] And for their sakes I sanctify Myself,
so that they also may be sanctified by the truth.

JESUS PRAYS FOR ALL BELIEVERS

[20] " I pray not only for these, but also for those who
believe in Me through their message;
[21] that they all may be one, just as You, Father, are in
Me, and I in You; that in Us they also may be one,
so that the world may believe that You sent Me.
[22] And the glory which You have given to Me
I have given to them,
that they may be one just as We are one:
[23] I in them and You in Me; so that they may be
made perfect in one, and that the world may know
that You sent Me and have loved them
just as You have loved Me.

[24] " Father, I desire that they also whom You have
given Me may be with Me where I am, so that
they may see My glory which You have given Me;
because You loved Me
before the founding of the world.

[25] "Righteous Father!
The world has not known You, but I have known
You; and these have known that You sent Me.

John 17:20. This is one of the most encouraging verses in the Bible. Jesus closes His time of teaching His friends (see note at 13:31) with a great prayer which reaches beyond the eleven to those who will believe in Him through their message. This prayer is for all believers of all time—including *you*. If you have believed in Him, Jesus' prayer is that His Father would lead you into a deeper knowledge of His love (verse 26).

²⁶ And I made Your Name known to them and will make it known, so that the love with which You have loved Me may be in them, and I in them."

JESUS BETRAYED AND ARRESTED

18 When Jesus had said these things, He went out with His disciples across the Kedron ravine, where there was a garden which He and His disciples entered. ² Now Judas, His betrayer, also knew the place, because Jesus often met there with His disciples. ³ So Judas took a detachment of soldiers and some temple police from the chief priests and Pharisees, and came there with lanterns, torches, and weapons. ⁴ Then Jesus, knowing everything that was going to happen to Him, went out and said to them,

"Who is it you're looking for?"

⁵ "Jesus the Nazarene," they answered Him.

"I am He," Jesus told them.

And Judas, His betrayer, was also standing with them. ⁶ So when He told them, "I am He," they shrank back and fell to the ground. ⁷ Then He asked them again,

"Who is it you're looking for?"

"Jesus the Nazarene," they said.

⁸ "I told you that I am He," Jesus replied. "So if you're looking for Me, let these men go." ⁹ This was to fulfill the statement which He had made:

"Of those You have given Me I have not lost one."

¹⁰ Then Simon Peter, who had a sword, drew it, struck the high priest's servant, and cut off his right ear. (The servant's name was Malchus.) ¹¹ So Jesus said to Peter,

"Sheathe your sword! Shall I not drink the cup which the Father has given Me?"

JESUS APPEARS BEFORE ANNAS

¹² Then the detachment of soldiers, the captain, and the Jewish temple police arrested Jesus and tied Him up. ¹³ They first led Him away to Annas, for he was the father-in-law of Caiaphas, who was high priest that year. ¹⁴ Now it was Caiaphas who had advised the Jews that it was advantageous that one man should die for the people.

PETER DENIES HIS LORD

¹⁵ Meanwhile Simon Peter was following Jesus, as was the other disciple. Now that disciple was an acquaintance of the high priest, so he went into the high priest's courtyard with Jesus. ¹⁶ But Peter was standing outside by the door. So the other disciple, who was an acquaintance of the high priest, went out and spoke to the girl who kept the door, and brought Peter in. ¹⁷ Then the servant-girl who kept the door said to Peter,

"You aren't one of this man's disciples too, are you?"

"I am not!" he said. ¹⁸ Now the servants and the temple police had made a charcoal fire, because it was cold, and they were standing there warming themselves. Peter also was standing with them and warming himself.

JESUS ANSWERS THE HIGH PRIEST

¹⁹ Then the high priest questioned Jesus about His disciples and about His teaching. ²⁰ Jesus answered him,

"I have spoken openly to the world. I have always taught in synagogues and in the temple courts, where the Jews always congregate, and I have spoken nothing in secret. ²¹ Why do you question Me? Question those who heard what I told them. Look, they know what I said!" ²² And when He had said these things, one of the temple police standing by slapped Jesus' face, saying,

²³ "Is that any way to answer the high priest?"

"If I have spoken wrongly," Jesus answered him, "give evidence about the wrong; but if rightly, why do you hit Me?"

²⁴ Annas sent Him bound to Caiaphas the high priest.

PETER DENIES HIS LORD TWICE MORE

²⁵ Now Simon Peter was standing and warming himself. So they said to him,

"You aren't one of His disciples too, are you?"

Then he denied it and said,

"I am not!"

²⁶ One of the high priest's servants, a relative of the man whose ear Peter had cut off, said,

"Didn't I see you with Him in the garden?"

²⁷ Then Peter denied it again, and at once a rooster crowed.

Jesus' Trial Before Pilate

²⁸ So they took Jesus from Caiaphas to the governor's headquarters, and it was early morning. But they did not enter the headquarters themselves, in order that they might not be defiled, but might eat the Passover.

²⁹ Then Pilate came out to them and said,

"What charge do you bring against this man?"

³⁰ In reply, they said to him,

"If this man were not a criminal, we would not have handed Him over to you."

³¹ So Pilate told them,

"You take Him yourselves and judge Him according to your law."

Therefore the Jews said to him,

"It's not lawful for us to put anyone to death." ³² This was to fulfill the statement of Jesus, which He made to indicate what sort of death He was going to die. ³³ Then Pilate went back into the headquarters, called Jesus, and said to Him,

"Are You the King of the Jews?"

³⁴ Jesus answered him,

"Are you saying this on your own, or have others told you about Me?"

³⁵ Pilate replied,

"I'm not a Jew, am I? Your own nation and the chief priests handed You over to me. What have You done?"

³⁶ "My kingdom is not of this world," Jesus answered. "If My kingdom were of this world, My servants would fight, so that I wouldn't be handed over to the Jews. But in fact My kingdom does not have its source here."

³⁷ So Pilate said to Him,

"You are a king then?"

"You say that I am a king," Jesus replied. "For this I was born, and for this I have come into the world, to testify to the truth. Everyone who is of the truth listens to My voice."

³⁸ Pilate said to Him,

"What is truth?"

JESUS OR BARABBAS?

And when he had said this, he went out to the Jews again and told them, "I find absolutely no grounds for charging Him. [39] But you have a custom that I release one man to you at the Passover. So do you want me to release the King of the Jews for you?" [40] Then they all shouted back,

"Not this fellow, but Barabbas!" Now Barabbas was a bandit.

JESUS FLOGGED AND MOCKED

19 So then Pilate took Jesus and had Him flogged. [2] Also the soldiers twisted a crown out of thorns and put it on His head. And they threw a purple robe around Him [3] and kept saying,

"Hail, King of the Jews!" And they kept slapping His face.

[4] Pilate then went out again and said to them,

"Look, I'm bringing Him out to you, so that you may know that I find absolutely no grounds for charging Him."

PILATE PERSUADED TO CRUCIFY JESUS

[5] Then Jesus came out wearing the crown of thorns and the purple robe. And Pilate* said to them,

"Look! The man!"

[6] So when the chief priests and the temple police saw Him, they shouted,

"Crucify! Crucify Him!"

Pilate told them,

"Take Him and crucify Him yourselves, because I find no grounds for charging Him."

[7] "We have a law," the Jews answered him, "and according to our law He must die, because He made Himself the Son of God." [8] So when Pilate heard this statement, he was more afraid than ever. [9] Then he went back into the headquarters again, and said to Jesus,

"Where are You from?" But Jesus gave him no answer. [10] So Pilate said to Him, "Aren't You speaking to *me?* Don't You know that I have authority to crucify You and authority to release You?"

[11] "You would have no authority over Me at all," Jesus replied, "if it hadn't been given to you from above. Therefore, the one who handed Me over to you has the greater sin." [12] From that

moment Pilate kept trying to release Him. But the Jews shouted,

"If you release this fellow, you aren't Caesar's friend. Everyone who sets himself up as king opposes Caesar!" [13] So when Pilate heard this statement, he brought Jesus outside. And he sat down on the judge's bench in a place called The Stone Pavement, but in Hebrew, *Gabbatha*. [14] Now it was the day of Preparation for the Passover, and it was about six a.m. Then he said to the Jews,

"Look! Your king!"

[15] But they shouted,

"Take Him away! Take Him away! Crucify Him!"

Pilate said to them,

"Shall I crucify *your king?*"

"We have no king but Caesar!" the chief priests answered. [16] So then he handed Him over to them to be crucified.

THE CRUCIFIXION

They took Jesus and led Him away. [17] And carrying His cross, He went out to an area called Skull Place, which in Hebrew is called *Golgotha*. [18] There they crucified Him, and two others with Him, one on either side, with Jesus in the middle. [19] Pilate also had a sign lettered and put on the cross. And the inscription was:

> **JESUS THE NAZARENE**
> **THE KING OF THE JEWS.**

[20] Therefore many of the Jews read this sign, because the place where Jesus was crucified was near the city, and it was written in Hebrew, Greek, and Latin. [21] Then the Jewish chief priests said to Pilate,

"Don't write, 'The King of the Jews,' but, 'This fellow said, "I am the King of the Jews."' "

[22] Pilate replied,

"What I have written, I have written!"

[23] So when the soldiers had crucified Jesus, they took His clothes and divided them into four parts, a part for each soldier. They also took the tunic, but the tunic was seamless, woven in one piece from the top. [24] So they said to one another,

"Let's not tear it, but toss for it, to see who gets it." This was to fulfill the Scripture which says:

*"They divided My clothes among themselves,
And for My clothing they cast lots."*

So the soldiers did these things.

JESUS PROVIDES FOR HIS MOTHER

[25] Meanwhile, standing by the cross of Jesus were His mother, and His mother's sister, Mary the wife of Clopas, and Mary of Magdala. [26] So when Jesus saw His mother and the disciple whom He loved standing by, He said to His mother,

"Woman, there is your son!" [27] Then He said to the disciple, "There is your mother!" And from that hour the disciple took her into his home.

THE FINISHED WORK OF CHRIST

[28] After this, when He saw that everything was now accomplished, in fulfillment of Scripture, Jesus said,

"I'm thirsty!" [29] Now a vessel full of sour wine was sitting there; and they filled a sponge with sour wine, fixed it on a stalk of hyssop, and held it up to His mouth. [30] So when Jesus had received the sour wine, He said,

"It is finished!"

And bowing His head, He yielded up His spirit.

A SOLDIER PIERCES JESUS' SIDE

[31] Therefore, since it was the Preparation Day, so that the bodies might not remain on the cross on the Sabbath (for that Sabbath was a high day), the Jews requested Pilate that the legs of the men might be broken, and that they might be taken away. [32] So the soldiers came and broke the legs of the first man and of the other one who had been crucified with Him. [33] But when they came to Jesus they did not break His legs, since they saw He was already dead. [34] But one of the soldiers pierced His side with a spear, and at once blood and water came out.

[35] Now he who saw this has testified, so that you may believe. And his testimony is true, and he knows he is telling the truth. [36] For these things happened so that the Scripture would be fulfilled:

"Not one of His bones shall be broken."
And again another Scripture says:
"They shall look on Him whom they pierced."

THE BURIAL OF CHRIST

[38] After these things, Joseph of Arimathea, who was a disciple of Jesus, but secretly for fear of the Jews, asked Pilate that he might remove the body of Jesus. So Pilate gave permission. Then he came and removed the body of Jesus. [39] Now Nicodemus (who had come to Jesus the first time at night) also came, bringing a mixture of about 100 pounds of myrrh and aloes. [40] So they took Jesus' body and wrapped it in linen strips with the aromatic spices, according to the burial custom of the Jews. [41] Now at the place where He was crucified there was a garden, and in the garden a new tomb in which no one had yet been interred. [42] So there they placed Jesus, since the tomb was nearby, because of the Jewish Preparation Day.

PETER AND JOHN AT THE EMPTY TOMB

20 Now on the first day of the week Mary of Magdala came to the tomb early, while it was still dark. And she saw that the stone had been removed from the tomb. [2] So she ran and went to Simon Peter, and to the other disciple, whom Jesus loved, and told them,

"They have taken away my Lord out of the tomb, and we don't know where they have put Him!" [3] Then Peter and the other disciple went out, heading for the tomb. [4] Now the two were running together, and the other disciple outran Peter and got to the tomb first. [5] Stooping down, he saw the linen wrappings lying there, but he did not go in. [6] Then, following him, came Simon Peter. And he went into the tomb and saw the linen wrappings lying there, [7] but the handkerchief which had been on His head was folded up in a separate place by itself, not lying with the linen wrappings. [8] So then the other disciple, who had reached the tomb first, went into the tomb. And he saw and believed. [9] For they did not yet know the Scripture, that He had to rise from the dead. [10] So the disciples went home again.

MARY OF MAGDALA SEES THE RISEN LORD

[11] But Mary stood outside, opposite the tomb, crying. Then, as she was crying, she stooped to look into the tomb. [12] And she saw two angels in white sitting there, one at the head and one at the feet, where Jesus' body had been lying. [13] And they said to her,

"Woman, why are you crying?"

"Because they have taken away my Lord," she told them, "and I don't know where they have put Him." [14] And having said this, she turned around and saw Jesus standing there. But she did not know that it was Jesus.

[15] "Woman," Jesus said to her, "why are you crying? Who is it you're looking for?"

Supposing that it was the gardener, she said to Him, "Sir, if you have removed Him, tell me where you have put Him, and I will take Him away."

[16] Jesus said to her,

"Mary!"

Turning around, she said to Him,

"Rabboni!" (which means Teacher).

[17] "Don't cling to Me," Jesus told her, "since I have not yet ascended to My Father. But go to My brothers and tell them, 'I am ascending to My Father and your Father—My God and your God.'"

[18] Mary of Magdala went to report to the disciples that she had seen the Lord and He had told her these things.

THE DISCIPLES COMMISSIONED

[19] When it was evening on that day, the first day of the week, and the doors were locked where the disciples were assembled for fear of the Jews, Jesus came and stood among them. And He said to them,

"Peace to you!" [20] And having said this He showed them His hands and His side. So the disciples were overjoyed when they saw the Lord. [21] Jesus said to them again, "Peace to you! Just as the Father has sent Me, I also send you." [22] Having said this He breathed on them and said to them, "Receive the Holy Spirit. [23] If you forgive the sins of any, they are forgiven them; if you retain the sins of any, they are retained."

THOMAS SEES AND BELIEVES

²⁴ But one of the Twelve, Thomas (called Twin), was not with them when Jesus came. ²⁵ So the other disciples kept telling him,

"We have seen the Lord!"

But he said to them,

"If I don't see the nailprints in His hands, put my finger into the nailprints, and put my hand into His side, I will *not* believe!"

²⁶ So after eight days the disciples were indoors again, and Thomas was with them. Jesus came, even though the doors were locked, and stood among them. And He said,

"Peace to you!"

²⁷ Then He said to Thomas,

"Put your finger here and observe My hands. Reach out your hand and put it into My side. And don't be unbelieving but believing!"

²⁸ And Thomas answered and said to Him,

"My Lord and My God!"

²⁹ "Because you have seen Me,"* Jesus told him, "you have believed. Blessed are those who have not seen, and yet have believed!"

JOHN'S PURPOSE IN WRITING THIS BOOK

³⁰ Jesus actually performed many other miraculous signs in the presence of His disciples, which are not written in this book. ³¹ But these are written so that you may believe that Jesus is the Christ, the Son of God, and that by believing you may have life in His Name.

John 20:30-31. Read these verses carefully to refresh your memory regarding John's purpose for writing. He wants you to believe that Jesus is the Christ. That is, he wants you to believe that Jesus is the Savior who gives eternal life to every single person who believes in Him.

Becoming a Christian does not depend on joining a church, walking an aisle, making some commitment to God, or making some change in your life. As you can tell after reading John's Gospel, having eternal life depends on believing in Christ. John guarantees that when we believe that Jesus is the Christ we have eternal life. Have you believed? If not, what better way to close your reading of this book than by believing in the Savior, of whom John speaks, the Lord Jesus Christ?

BREAKFAST BY BLUE GALILEE

21 After these things Jesus revealed Himself again to His disciples by Lake Tiberias, and He revealed Himself in this way:

² Simon Peter, Thomas (called Twin), Nathanael from Cana of Galilee, Zebedee's sons, and two others of His disciples were together.

³ "I'm going fishing!" Simon Peter said to them.

"We're coming with you," they told him. Off they went and got into the boat. Yet that night they caught nothing.

⁴ But when daybreak had now come, Jesus stood on the beach. The disciples, though, did not know that it was Jesus.

⁵ "Boys," Jesus said to them, "you don't have any fish, do you?"

"No," they answered Him.

⁶ "Cast the net on the right side of the boat," He told them, "and you'll find some." So they did, and they were unable to haul it in because of the large number of fish. ⁷ Therefore the disciple whom Jesus loved said to Peter,

"It's the Lord!" When Simon Peter heard that it was the Lord, he put on his outer garment (for he was stripped), and plunged into the lake. ⁸ But the other disciples came in the boat, dragging the net with fish (since they weren't far from land, but about 100 yards off). ⁹ So when they got out on land they saw a charcoal fire ready, with fish lying on it, and bread.

¹⁰ "Bring some of the fish you've just caught," Jesus told them. ¹¹ Simon Peter went up and dragged the net onto the land, full of large fish—153 of them. And even though there were so many, the net was not torn.

¹² "Come and have breakfast," Jesus told them. But none of the disciples dared ask Him, "Who are You?" because they knew it was the Lord. ¹³ So Jesus came and took the bread and gave it to them, and likewise the fish.

¹⁴ This was now the third time Jesus appeared to His disciples after He was raised from the dead.

JESUS REINSTATES PETER

¹⁵ So when they had eaten breakfast, Jesus asked Simon Peter,

"Simon, son of Jonah,* do you love me more than these?"

"Yes, Lord," he said to Him, "You know that I'm fond of You."

"Feed my lambs!" He told him.

¹⁶ A second time he asked him, "Simon, son of Jonah, do you love Me?"

"Yes, Lord," he said to Him, "You know that I'm fond of You."

"Shepherd My sheep!" He told him. ¹⁷ He asked him the third time, "Simon, son of Jonah, are you fond of Me?"

Peter was grieved that He asked him the third time, "Are you fond of Me?" And he said to Him, "Lord, You know everything! You know that I'm fond of You."

"Feed My sheep!" Jesus told him.

¹⁸ "Amen, amen,* I tell you: When you were young you used to fasten your belt and walk wherever you wanted. But when you grow old you will stretch out your hands and someone else will fasten a belt around you and carry you where you don't want to go." ¹⁹ In saying this He was indicating the kind of death by which he would glorify God. After saying this, He told him,

"Follow Me!"

THE BELOVED DISCIPLE AND HIS BOOK

²⁰ Then Peter turned around and saw the disciple whom Jesus loved following, the one who had leaned against His heart at the supper and asked, "Lord, who's the one that's going to betray You?" ²¹ When Peter saw him he said to Jesus,

"But Lord, what about *him?*"

²² "If I want him to remain till I come," Jesus told him, "what is that to you? *You* follow Me!"

²³ So this report spread to the brothers, that this disciple would not die. Yet Jesus had not told him that he would not die, but, "If I want him to remain till I come, what is that to you?"

EPILOGUE

²⁴ This is the disciple who testifies to these things and wrote them down; and we know that his testimony is true.

²⁵ Yes, there are also many other things that Jesus did, which, if they were written one by one, I don't suppose even the world itself could contain the books that would be written!

Amen.

CONCLUDING NOTES

Do You Believe?

It is impossible to miss John's emphasis on believing in the Son of God. Again and again, this disciple of Christ repeated his crucial theme: "Whoever believes in the Son has eternal life; but whoever disbelieves the Son will not see life, but God's wrath remains upon him" (John 3:36).

John has presented his Lord as a Savior worthy of your belief. Do you believe John's testimony about Jesus? Or, don't you? "Whoever believes in Him is not judged, but whoever does not believe is already judged, because he has not believed in the Name of the only begotten Son of God" (John 3:18).

When you believe that He is who He claims to be (the Christ) and that He gives eternal life to everyone who believes this claim, then you have that life. "For God so loved the world that He gave His only begotten Son, so that whoever believes in Him will not perish, but have eternal life" (John 3:16). It's very important that you understand you cannot save yourself. Jesus Christ must be the only object of your faith. You are a Christian when you can say confidently, "I have eternal life because I believe in Jesus Christ."

Let's Review

John has shown the importance of looking to Jesus alone for eternal life. God sent Jesus, His Son, to die on the Cross for our sins. When you believe in Him, you have eternal life and you can know that He will keep His promise never to lose you and that He will raise you up in the resurrection to live with Him forever (John 6:40). This fact, that one's eternal salvation is totally dependent upon Jesus and His work on the Cross, brings joy to every new believer in Him.

God loves you so much He does not want you to lose this joy. That's why He inspired John to repeat that truth countless times in this book. Be careful not to begin looking within yourself for continued assurance of this fact. Christians who do this invariably lose their joy. Your feelings as a new Christian will probably change daily. Most Christians experience some feelings of doubt or confusion concerning their new life as a child of God. But the facts of God's Word are unchanging and absolutely reliable.

Many verses from John have reminded believers of the joy of their salvation, but one promise has been especially comforting. In John 5:24 Jesus pledged, " . . . whoever hears My word and believes the One who sent Me has eternal life, and will not come into judgment, but has passed from death to life."

This verse contains one condition and three results. *If* I trust in God's promise concerning Jesus, *then* (1) I have eternal life, (2) I will not come into judgment, and (3) I have passed from death to life.

Note the careful wording of Christ's statement. There should be no doubt: Those who hear His message and believe already have eternal life, will not be judged for their sin, and have already begun their new life.

Have you understood the message of John? Have you believed that Jesus is telling the truth when He claims to be the Son of God who gives eternal life to everyone who believes in Him? Then you can claim this precious promise from the Lord Jesus Christ Himself. Regardless of how you feel or what people may say, you *have* eternal life.

What Now?

Now that you are a Christian there are several things which will help you grow in your spiritual life. We would recommend that you begin this growth today by:

1. Praying (talking to God) daily.
2. Reading the Bible daily. We suggest you start with the Book of Philippians, then Romans. Later, you might want to read through the whole New Testament starting with the Book of Matthew.

3. Finding and getting involved in a Bible-believing church which stresses the free gift of eternal life.

4. Finding a Christian friend to talk with for encouragement and support.

5. Telling others about your new life in Christ and the gift of eternal life to all who believe in Him.

FOR FURTHER READING

A Word about the Translation and Text

Logos 21 is translated from *The Greek New Testament According to the Majority Text*, edited by Zane C. Hodges and Arthur L. Farstad (Nashville: Thomas Nelson Publishers, 2d ed., 1985). *Logos* is the Greek word for *word* (see John 1:1) and the *21* means we are seeking to bring that word, or message from God, into the 21st century.

John wrote his Gospel in everyday language (*koiné* or common Greek). Our translation is modern, easy to read, and yet an accurate representation of his original. Where English usage allows, the translation is fairly literal; where it does not, a freer rendering is used.

In Logos 21, *italics* show emphasis. What is emphasized is often clear in Greek by word order or other means, but not obvious in English without occasional italics. Logos 21 also uses italics for foreign words (such as *rabboni*) and to indicate direct quotations from the Old Testament.

Whereas most modern versions are based on a text heavily influenced by scholars who have largely disregarded or discounted the *majority* of Greek manuscripts, Logos 21 represents the vast bulk of existing Greek manuscripts. It is similar to the traditional text used by William Tyndale (1526) and the King James translators (1611), but corrected by later finds.

The Majority Text used here represents from 80–95% of our Greek manuscripts. These stem largely from the areas which first received the original Gospels and Epistles (modern Greece and Turkey). On the whole, these manuscripts have a remarkable agreement among themselves. Heavy reliance on the few older manuscripts, mostly from Egypt (the region dry enough to preserve ancient papyrus), seems unwarranted to us. These manuscripts, often called "Alexandrian," have many discrepancies between them. Also, no New Testament book, as far as we know, was originally sent to Egypt, the area where these manuscripts likely originated.

Those who wish to pursue this subject further should read Wilbur Pickering's *The Identity of the New Testament Text*, 2d ed. 1977; and Harry A. Sturz's *The Byzantine Text Type and New Testament Textual Criticism*, 1984, both from Thomas Nelson Publishers.

Also, for further information write to: The Executive Secretary, The Majority Text Society, Box 141289, Dallas, TX 75214-1289, U.S.A.

NOTES ON THE TEXT

Except for "Amen, amen," verses marked * are places where there is a significant variation between the Majority Text, which we follow, and the so-called "critical text," abbreviated "NU." NU is an abbreviation for the Greek text published in Nestle-Aland's 27th edition and the United Bible Societies' 4th edition (virtually identical texts, different apparatuses [footnotes]).

In each case, the reading in Logos 21 has the support of a large majority of manuscripts.

• **1:18** The Majority Text reads "only begotten *Son*" and the NU reads "only begotten *God*." John's style supports "Son," the traditional reading, occurring also in 3:16, 18, and 1 John 4:9. The word "begotten" goes much better with the Father–Son relationship concept than the Father–God relationship.

• **1:42** The Majority reading "son of *Jonah*" agrees with Peter's father's name in Matthew 16:17, where all agree *Jonah* is the correct reading. The committee producing the commentary on the NU text maintains the discrepancy was original and was changed to make it agree with Matthew (also in John 21:15-17). We believe the change was *from* Jonah, the true name of Peter's father, and was probably accidental.

• **1:51** Though John wrote in Greek, he kept our Lord's unique Hebrew expression "Amen, amen" untranslated. There is no suitable literal translation, so the versions differ ("Verily, verily," "truly, truly," "most assuredly," etc.). The word *amen*, which comes from the Hebrew verb for *believe* (as in Genesis 15:6), means "so be it" or "it is firm." In the 4th century when Bible scholar Jerome translated the famous Latin Vulgate he also left the exact words Jesus used. Following John and Jerome, we have done the same.

• 3:3, 5, 11 See note to 1:51.

• 3:13 The NU text omits "who is in Heaven," though it has good support. The Majority inclusion supports the doctrine of the omnipresence of the Second Person of the Trinity, even while on earth in the Incarnation. The NU committee sees this orthodox reading as a later christological development, a viewpoint consistent with liberal theology.

• 4:6 Or, about noon if John is using Jewish time.

• 5:2 The Majority reads *Bethesda*. NU reads *Bethzatha*, supported by only two manuscripts (4th century and 10th century A.D.). The 1st century Copper Scroll from Qumran supports the traditional *Bethesda*. The choice of *Bethzatha* by the NU committee introduces a historical error into the text.

• 5:3b-4 The part of v. 3 starting with "waiting" through v. 4 is omitted in NU text. The statement in v. 7 seems to demand inclusion of the passage, since without it the verse would be extremely obscure. Ancient evidence for inclusion comes from Tatian's *Diatessaron* (2d century) and Tertullian (3d century). These balance the omission in the "Alexandrian" manuscripts.

• 5:19, 24, 25 See note to 1:51.

• 6:26, 32, 47, 53 See note to 1:51.

• 6:47 NU's omission of Jesus' words "in Me" makes His statement on how to have eternal life quite vague: What or whom does one need to believe in for eternal life?

• 7:8 NU's omission of "yet" tends to portray Jesus as a liar, since in v. 10 He *does* go to the festival. "Yet" is not only in the majority of manuscripts, but also in early papyri. The NU committees did recognize the early inclusion of "yet," but said it was introduced after the original to "alleviate the inconsistency."

• 7:53–8:11 This is the main textual problem in John. The oldest Greek manuscripts we have lack the passage, but the vast majority (over 900 carefully examined mss., plus several hundred others) contains it. The 4th century Latin Vulgate contains it too. *John's style* within the disputed passage includes: (1) "they said this to test Him" in 8:6 (cf. John 6:6; 7:39; 11:51; 12:6, 33; and 21:19); (2) the vocative (direct address) use of "woman" in 8:10 (cf. John 2:4; 4:21; 19:26, and 20:13, 15); and (3) "don't sin any more" in 8:11, which only occurs one other time in the NT (John 5:14). Also, if one reads the preceding and following context *without* the disputed passage, it is clear that the subject abruptly changes from "they," the Pharisees, in 7:52, to Jesus in 8:12. Also, in 8:12 Jesus speaks to them "again," which supports that He was speaking in the immediately preceding context.

If, as we believe, the passage is authentic, why would the Alexandrian manuscripts omit it? Leading church father and theologian, Augustine, (about A.D. 430) answers: "Certain persons of little faith, or rather enemies of the true faith, fearing, I suppose, lest their wives should be given impunity in sinning, removed from their manuscripts the Lord's acts of forgiveness toward the adulteress, as if He who said 'sin no more' had granted permission to sin." (See Augustine, "Adulterous Marriages" [2.7] trans. by Charles T. Huegelmeyer, in *Saint Augustine: Treatises on Marriage and Other Subjects* [New York: Fathers of the Church, 1955], p. 107.)

• 8:34, 51, 58 See note to 1:51.

• 9:35 NU reads "Son of *Man*" for "Son of *God*." Both are titles of the Messiah, but the title expressing Deity fits the context better since no man had ever cured blindness from birth before. Also, while Luke stresses Christ's humanity, John highlights His Deity.

• 10:1, 7 See note to 1:51.

• 12:24 See note to 1:51.

• 13:16, 20, 21, 38 See note to 1:51.

• 14:12 See note to 1:51.

• 14:15 NU text reads "you will keep," a *prediction* of compliance; the Majority Text reads "keep," a *command* to those who love the Lord—who sometimes fail to do so.

• 16:20, 23 See note to 1:51.

• 19:5 Literally "he (or He) said." It's possible that Jesus Himself said this since *Jesus* is the nearest antecedent.

• 20:29 TR ("Textus Receptus" or "Received Text") adds "Thomas," but neither the oldest nor Majority supports this reading.

• 21:15-17 See note to 1:42.

• 21:18 See note to 1:51.

CREDITS

The original translator of most of the chapters of John in Logos 21 and the general editor is **Arthur L. Farstad**. He started the work in 1984 soon after finishing his assignment as Executive Editor of the New King James Version of the Bible. Dr. Farstad is a graduate of Washington Bible College and has advanced degrees in Hebrew and Greek from Dallas Theological Seminary, where he taught NT Greek for five and a half years. He is also one of the editors of *The NKJV Greek-English Interlinear*.

Nova-Scotia-born-and-bred **William H. McDowell** was the English editor of the NKJV and has a similar role in this translation. Dr. McDowell is a graduate of the University of Toronto, Westminister Theological Seminary, Rollins College in Orlando, Florida, and has a doctorate from Toccoa Falls College in Georgia.

Zane C. Hodges was the co-editor with Dr. Farstad of *The Greek New Testament According to the Majority Text*, from which this translation was made. He is a graduate of Wheaton College and Dallas Theological Seminary, where he taught Greek for 27 years. He co-edited most of the Gospel of John with the general editor.

International evangelist **Frank D. Carmical**, a graduate of Houston Baptist University and Dallas Theological Seminary, has published a Christian novel, *The Omega Reunion*, and several short stories. He worked closely with the general editor on phraseology and vocabulary choices in John.

A few chapters were initially translated by Brazilian-born **Dr. Wilbur N. Pickering**, a Wycliffe missionary with a Th.M. from Dallas Theological Seminary and a Ph.D. in linguistics from the University of Toronto, and by **Dr. Robert N. Wilkin**, a graduate of the University of California at Irvine, who has a Ph.D. from Dallas Theological Seminary in New Testament.

Curtis Vaughan, one of the seven members of the Executive Review Committee of the NKJV New Testament and general editor of *The New Testament from 26 Translations*, carefully annotated this entire translation with many helpful suggestions for the final text. Dr. Vaughan is a veteran of 44 years of teaching Greek at Southwestern Baptist Theological Seminary in Ft. Worth, Texas. He is a graduate of Union University in Jackson, Tennessee and has both an M.Div. and a Th.D. from Southwestern.

The textual notes were written by **James F. Davis**, a doctoral student at Dallas Theological Seminary in New Testament. He is a graduate of the University of Wisconsin and Capital Bible Seminary in Washington D.C.

ABSOLUTELY FREE

INCORPORATED

P.O. Box 2 • Glide, Oregon 97443
Tel (541) 496-3046 • Fax (541)496-0304

Published by Absolutely Free Incorporated
Visit our Web Site at:
http://www.livingwater.org